I0418420

Souls Entwined

The Journey of Souls and Soulmates

Gideon Paull

Paull

Copyright © 2024 by Gideon Paull

All rights reserved.

No portion of this book may be reproduced in any form without written permission from the publisher or author, except as permitted by U.S. copyright law.

This publication is designed to provide accurate and authoritative information in regard to the subject matter covered. It is sold with the understanding that neither the author nor the publisher is engaged in rendering legal, investment, accounting or other professional services. While the publisher and author have used their best efforts in preparing this book, they make no representations or warranties with respect to the accuracy or completeness of the contents of this book and specifically disclaim any implied warranties of merchantability or fitness for a particular purpose. No warranty may be created or extended by sales representatives or written sales materials. The advice and strategies contained herein may not be suitable for your situation. You should consult with a professional when appropriate. Neither the publisher nor the author shall be liable for any loss of profit or any other commercial damages, including but not limited to special, incidental, consequential, personal, or other damages.

First Edition 2024

Illustrations by Gideon Paull

Printed in the United States of America

ISBN: 979-8-9887973-4-0

Dedicated to my soul mate, my one true love,
my inspiration and
the one I always find in every life.

Contents

Gender, God, and Pronouns

This book is intended for everyone, whatever your gender designation, religious affiliation, or no affiliation. It is difficult to speak about the soul and the spirit without addressing religion and God; while it is heavy in Judeo-Christian sources, it is agnostic when it comes to religion and should not be considered to favor one religious theology over another. As such, this book uses the words "God," "Higher Power," and "Divine" interchangeably to refer to any God-like entities. Likewise, the book doesn't identify God as any specific gender. Instead of using the pronoun "He," we don't identify the Higher Power with any specific gender and instead use the capitalized third-person pronouns "They/Them/Their."

Preface

What is genuine spirituality, and how can we achieve it?

"You don't go to a place of worship to find God. God will be found in your heart." Someone told me this when I confided in them that I struggled to connect with God through the prayers in the synagogue.

For years, I struggled to feel spiritually connected during my time in the synagogue. I often wondered why others seemed to find meaning in the prayers, the melodies, and the rituals, while I was met with silence. I asked myself, "Is it too much to hope for a real connection with the Divine? If others can find it through prayer, why can't I?"

On the surface, I appeared fully engaged, going through the motions of devotion during the three daily prayer services. But deep down, I felt disconnected. Despite my efforts, the sacred words and melodies didn't bridge the gap between me and a sense of God's presence. I felt lost, even in the midst of the congregation's passionate worship.

Judaism, however, is much more than the prayers recited in a synagogue. It's a way of life, a culture shaped by centuries of sacred teachings and interpretations. The prayers and rituals, rooted in ancient texts, carry a profound history. But for me, the synagogue wasn't the place where I found a connection to the Divine. My soul longed for something beyond structured worship, something more personal and transformative.

Judaism's foundation lies in the Torah, the timeless teachings of Moses. Over the centuries, those teachings have grown into a living faith, expressed through the mitzvot (commandments) and oral traditions like the Talmud. With the end of Temple worship, Judaism evolved into a faith that infused holiness into daily life. From celebrating the Sabbath and festivals to observing dietary laws and moral principles, Judaism became a faith that reaches beyond sacred spaces into every moment of a Jewish person's life.

A Journey of Spiritual Discovery

Growing up in Windsor, England—famous for its castle and royal history—my Jewish family stood out. Unlike areas with large Jewish communities, where synagogues, kosher shops, and schools support a Jewish lifestyle, Windsor offered no such resources. Being one of only a few Jewish families meant that our faith had to be nurtured at home, without the reinforcement of a broader community. We kept our traditions alive in a place mostly unaware of our customs, making us rely on our own creativity and commitment.

My mother led this effort, carefully balancing tradition with the practical realities of our environment. Our Judaism was observant, yet flexible. For example, we drove to synagogue on the Sabbath, which is traditionally not allowed. At home, we observed kosher rules, like waiting three hours between meat and dairy and eating only kosher meat. But outside, we allowed ourselves to be more lenient. My parents' approach showed that it's possible to honor Jewish tradition while engaging with the wider world. They taught us who we were and helped us stay true to our heritage even in a non-Jewish setting.

We were English in many respects—speaking the same language, attending the same schools, playing the same games—but we were also distinctly Jewish. Our faith came from the Torah and the commandments passed down through centuries, eventually forming daily religious practices that touched every part of life. After the Temple era ended, Judaism adapted, thriving not only in sacred spaces but in everyday moments, festivals, dietary laws, and moral conduct. This shift allowed Jewish life to survive and flourish everywhere.

From a young age, my parents made it clear that if I were to marry, it should be to someone Jewish. This wasn't just about religion—it was about keeping a lineage and tradition that had survived for thousands of years. For them, ensuring a Jewish spouse was about preserving this long, unbroken chain of heritage.

As I grew older, I dived into Orthodox Judaism, seeking a closer bond with God. I believed firmly in God but struggled with how to understand the divine essence. Although I saw successes in my life as signs of God's kindness, I found that strict Orthodoxy felt at odds with my heart. I learned that some teachings viewed other Jewish denominations as inferior and dismissed non-Jewish faiths, like Christianity and Islam, as misguided or harmful. This outlook eventually made me question the path I was on.

I realized that while I could recite prayers perfectly, I wasn't feeling a spiritual connection. The prayers were familiar, but they did not bring me closer to God. My faith in God never wavered, but it became clear that these well-known rituals and words weren't the right path for me to feel God's presence.

Over time, I relaxed my religious strictness but remained committed to Jewish holidays and traditions. Wherever I traveled, I sought out local Jewish communities for comfort and connection. In the United States, I joined a Conservative synagogue, enjoying the blend of tradition and modernity. But even there, I felt something missing spiritually. The services were structured, and the prayers were beautiful, yet I couldn't find the deep divine link I yearned for.

It was at this stage that Elaine entered my life. Upon learning she was a pastor, I impulsively said, "I don't believe in God," though that wasn't really true. Elaine saw through my words and recognized them as the cry of someone struggling to find a genuine spiritual bond. She was right—I believed in God, but I hadn't found the right way to connect.

Today, I still search for a direct link with the Divine, though not as intensely as before. I find spirituality in the life Elaine and I share, in our religious observances at home, our belief in God, her heartfelt prayers, and our many conversations about God's nature and will. God shows up unexpectedly when I need Them most, and I am grateful for being part of Their plan, sharing my life with Elaine as my wife and partner.

I've learned that genuine connection with God doesn't depend on one particular religious path. Religion is meant to guide us toward God, but if we get lost in rituals and rules, we can lose sight of the spiritual goal. Focusing too much on external practices can create exclusive circles, which I doubt is what a loving God wants. Would God favor one religion over another, or exclude those who worship differently?

I've found meaning in embracing diversity. Elaine and I differ in faith and practice, yet our differences enrich our spiritual journey and fit into a larger divine plan. Maybe God wants us to break down the walls that separate religions and cultures and come together as one human family.

Inclusion should replace exclusion, welcoming people of all faiths, cultures, colors, nationalities, sexual orientations, and beliefs. Together, we form a rich tapestry of humanity, united in seeking spirituality and fulfilling God's plan.

For me, Judaism is one path to God, just as Christianity is another, and many other religions may lead to the same spiritual destination. These religions are pathways, not the endpoint. I've chosen the Jewish path because it's my heritage, but it doesn't limit my connection to God.

My relationship with the Divine is deeply personal and always changing. God's presence is a constant within me, a divine spark that lives in everyone. We only need to recognize it to connect with God. Some do so through prayer or commandments, others through nature or music, and still others through quiet reflection. There's no wrong way. Every sincere effort to find God brings us closer to that sacred encounter.

A Soul-First Perspective

Religions around the world often mix together traditions and core beliefs so much that it's hard to tell them apart. For example, in Judaism, the idea that God gave Moses the Torah directly from above is closely tied to holiday traditions mentioned in it. Take the Passover Seder—it didn't just pop up out of nowhere. It grew and changed over thousands of years, guided by ancient scholars, until it became a deeply rooted part of Jewish practice. In Christianity, you've got something similar: while the doctrine of the Trinity focuses on the unity of the Father, Son, and Holy Spirit, traditions like Easter and Christmas have become shorthand for the Christian faith itself. I know from experience that it's easy to get swept up in these traditions and miss the deeper spiritual point.

Seeing people pushed to the margins because they don't follow certain religious rules made me question what "spirituality" even means within religion. In Judaism, I've watched communities show the door to those who don't believe the "right" things. In many branches of Christianity, there's this idea that if you don't believe in Jesus exactly as they say, you're out. That just doesn't fit with a Creator who gave every human being a spiritual soul and made us all in Their image. Everyone can tap into spirituality and be holy—no exceptions.

When I started looking at things from a soul-first perspective, I realized how far some religious rules and traditions have drifted from leading us toward anything truly divine. In thousands of years of religious evolution, people seem to have ended up going in circles spiritually.

Nowadays, fewer people show up at church or synagogue. The younger generations still believe in a Higher Power and want something spiritual, but they don't find it in these old structures. At the same time, we see more interfaith families blending different traditions, but often this just piles up rituals without uncovering deeper meaning.

We could do better than just haggling over which traditions to keep. Instead, we could shift our focus toward spiritual harmony and helping each other grow. We can keep our beloved traditions, but also inject them with genuine spiritual purpose. It's not about compromise or tossing everything out; it's about going above and beyond the old divisions and letting inclusivity and selflessness guide us.

This isn't easy. People cling to traditions because they're comfortable and familiar. But moving beyond "religion as usual" to find true spirituality doesn't mean dumping religion. It means reshaping it so that it echoes the divine qualities—kindness, compassion, restraint, and mercy—that can lift our souls and refine our earthly impulses. Doing this brings us closer to each other and to The Divine, getting us closer to that original vision: a world where humanity, supported by a spiritual soul, can thrive as if we're all living together in a renewed Garden of Eden.

In this book, I present a transformative paradigm: envisioning a world where we transcend religious divisions, uniting humanity with a shared spiritual purpose. I'm not suggesting abandoning or substituting established religions for new theologies. Instead, I advocate for an elevation beyond restrictive religious practices that might limit our spiritual growth. The focus here is to cultivate a spiritual life that aligns with the ultimate divine vision for humanity.

This work doesn't demand any religious commitment from its readers. You don't need to align with any particular faith to connect with its essence. At its core, this book offers a perspective rooted in the soul's experience, emphasizing spirituality over religious dogma. It endeavors to understand the expectations of a Higher Power from humanity, delving into the concept of a Universal God. This deity seeks communion with all of creation.

Centered on spirituality—the essence differentiating us from the animal kingdom—this work contemplates our purpose on Earth. It reflects on life, our existence, our experiences, and their underlying reasons. This work also encourages readers to question traditionally accepted religious principles.

In essence, this work serves as a guide to a rich, fulfilling existence, leading you toward a life marked by purpose and spiritual enrichment. It aims to usher you to that poignant moment at life's end where contentment reigns, allowing you to depart this realm with no lingering regrets. While it speaks of life, it's more aptly described as a guide to living purposefully and departing with peace.

Gideon Paull.
Los Angeles, December 2024

Chapter One

The Forbidden Love

Spiritual relationship is far more precious than physical. Physical relationship divorced from spiritual is body without soul. - Mahatma Gandhi

You know, a lot of people seem to figure out their spirituality pretty quickly, but for me, it's been a really long, messy journey. I've hit so many dead ends, walked alongside people who found their ultimate truth on paths that just didn't work for me, and had moments where I thought I'd finally figured myself out—only to lose it all again.

But over the years, I've learned a lot. And honestly, the biggest takeaway is that spirituality isn't a one-size-fits-all thing. It's different for everyone, and what works for one person might not even make sense to someone else.

The one thing I've really come to believe, though, is that people who treat religion as the same thing as spirituality are often the ones who try to push their beliefs and way of life onto others. It's like they can't separate their personal faith from the idea that everyone else needs to follow the same rules.

What's funny is that this whole thought came back to me recently in the most random way. It just hit me, out of nowhere, how much of a difference there is between discovering your own spirituality and just following someone else's religious roadmap. It's amazing how the smallest things can spark the biggest realizations.

One of my guilty pleasures is winding down at the end of the day with those easygoing TV shows—the kind you don't have to think too much about but can just enjoy for an hour or so of pure escapism. Recently, I stumbled upon a show called *Nobody Wants This*. It's about a rabbi named Noah—played by Adam Brody—who falls for a non-Jewish woman. *Oy*, what a scandal!

If Noah were an orthodox rabbi, strictly following all the commandments, this would've been a major scandal. But he's more of a gray area, somewhere between Conservative and Liberal Judaism. He observes some Jewish laws while simplifying others and not following some at all, though it's clear his Jewish identity is very important to him. Dating and eventually marrying a Jewish woman seemed like a non-negotiable for him—or at least, it was supposed to be.

But life doesn't always go according to plan. After a series of failed relationships with Jewish women, Noah meets Joanne—a relationship and sex podcaster played by Kristen Bell. Sparks fly instantly, and they connect on a deep, almost soulmate level. Of course, the drama unfolds predictably, with Noah's family strongly opposing the relationship. Thus the premise for the first season, and probably many more.

Aside from some uncanny parallels to my own life, I didn't give the show much thought—until I came across a TikTok (yes, another guilty pleasure of mine) featuring an Orthodox Jewish woman sharing her opinion on it. She said something along the lines of, *"It's obvious that someone who doesn't know true spirituality by keeping all the commandments would stray to forbidden love."* She went on to claim, *"The rabbi in this show isn't really Jewish; true Jews are only those that keep all the commandments and study Torah. That's true spirituality. and someone with true spirituality would never stray to forbidden love."*

Wow, there's so much to unpack from that super-opinionated 30-second TikTok. First off, the young woman clearly believes that spirituality can *only* be found in her specific, narrow practice of her religion. By saying that, she's essentially dismissing billions of people worldwide, implying they're somehow not "worthy" of true spirituality.

> *What does it really mean to be spiritual? And why does religion so often feel the need to co-opt spirituality, bending it to fit its own agenda?*

Here's the thing, though: I know plenty of people who follow more liberal or even Conservative branches of Judaism—people who don't adhere to strict Orthodox doctrine—who still find deep, genuine spirituality in their practice. And honestly, this isn't just about Judaism. If you take the same argument and shift it to any religion, the same logic applies. Every faith has its stricter interpretations and its more flexible ones, and the stricter groups often claim they have a monopoly on "real" spirituality.

So that's where my big question comes in: What *does* it really mean to be spiritual? And why does religion so often feel the need to co-opt spirituality, bending it to fit its own agenda? Is it about power? Control? Or maybe just the comfort of defining something that, at its core, is deeply personal and undefinable? Whatever the reason, it's a question that feels more relevant now than ever and one we will unpack before you're halfway through this book.

Love stories like the one in *'Nobody Wants This'* offer a glimpse into a utopia where barriers of culture, religion, nationality, and ethnicity dissolve, connecting us all through something profoundly universal. Yet, even within a single faith, the topic of intermarriage remains a source of tension, as differing interpretations of belief often collide.

The show's first season has only scratched the surface, with plenty of drama still to come. But I can't help imagining a future for Noah and Joanne where they overcome their cultural and religious divides—not by abandoning their identities or compromising their beliefs, but by finding a spiritual connection that goes beyond tradition.

In my vision, their love would allow them to honor their distinct heritages while enriching each other's lives through their unique perspectives. Together, they could show us that true compatibility doesn't demand conformity but thrives on understanding and respect. Their journey could be a powerful reminder that spiritual potential knows no boundaries and that a world without rigid divides is a world where love and connection flourish.

But love, no matter how deeply spiritual, doesn't exist in a bubble. We're all connected to family, friends, and society, and their expectations can't simply be ignored. For many interfaith couples, the rejection they face from loved ones is a painful reality. And in those moments, rejection tends to cut both ways—it strains not just the couple's relationship with their community but also their ties to each other. True spiritual harmony isn't just about the couple finding peace within themselves; it's about rebuilding bridges between those who feel left behind and those daring to step outside tradition.

> *The truth is, no single*
> *religion owns the path*
> *to enlightenment.*

That's no easy task. Personal spiritual growth is one thing, but asking others to set aside their biases and embrace shared humanity? That's an uphill climb.

Too often, religious and cultural norms box us in, narrowing our view of the world and keeping us from seeing the beauty in other faiths and traditions. The truth is that no single religion owns the path to enlightenment. There are many roads, and they all lead to the same destination: a deep, meaningful spirituality. But we waste so much energy defending our own beliefs, caught up in proving one theology "right" over another, that we lose sight of what really matters—living spiritually fulfilling lives.

Maybe stories like Noah and Joanne's are a gentle nudge, reminding us to shift our focus. Instead of fixating on what separates us, we can choose to embrace what unites us. Instead of clinging to rigid doctrines, we can grow together spiritually. In that shift, there's hope—not just for their fictional love story but for all of us in the real world, too.

We're often so quick to place labels on one another—*Black, White, Jewish, Christian, Asian, Latino*—as if those words alone could define the entirety of who we are. But imagine a world where we could look beyond those labels, where we'd strip away the layers of cultural and religious differences and connect soul to soul. In that space, we'd see one another's essence, unclouded by the identities we're assigned.

It's there, on that deeper level, where compatibility and understanding truly flourish. By recognizing the beauty in each other's souls, we might discover a connection that transcends all boundaries—a connection rooted in our shared humanity and a mutual desire for growth, love, and harmony. What a world that could be.

Could their relationship serve as a model for the kind of unity that a Higher Power envisions for humanity? How can we bring such a vision to life? Transcending above religion and cultural differences to find true spirituality doesn't suggest abandoning religion or age-old cherished traditions and rituals. Instead, it proposes honing our focus on clearly echoing the divine attributes, such as kindness, compassion, restraint, selflessness, love, and mercy. Embracing these virtues nurtures our souls, refines our worldly instincts, and strengthens our bond with humanity and the Divine.

By prioritizing spiritual altruism over strictly ritualistic religious practices, we not only find enriched ways to connect with The Divine but also embrace inclusivity over division. As we gravitate away from divisive religious doctrines, we adopt a more inclusive approach, shifting our perspectives.

When we perceive humanity through the lens of the spiritual soul, our traditions evolve. We don't abandon cherished customs; instead, we rejuvenate them with renewed purpose.

However, before we delve into defining this new paradigm of inclusiveness and spirituality before we begin to understand the amazing concepts of 'soul mates,' we must first understand what the nature of the soul and the spirit are, how they relate to religion, and how they influence us in our day-to-day lives.

The upcoming chapters will offer a deeper exploration of the forces that drive us as humans and our ultimate purpose on this earth. We'll endeavor to understand humanity and our reason for being, not through human eyes but rather through the lens of the soul and possibly through the eyes of the divine.

Chapter Two

The Tale of Two Souls and a Spirit

The best portion of a good man's life is his little, nameless, unremembered acts of kindness and of love. - William Wordsworth

The English cleric and leader of the Methodist revival movement within the Church of England, [1] John Wesley (1703 - 1791), used to ask people, "How is it with your soul?" When asking this question, Wesley was asking people to look at their lives and reflect on their choices. He held the belief that a person's outward manifestation, how they behaved in society, was a direct result of the health of that person's soul. The health

---

1. Wesley's teachings and the format of his small group meetings, known as class meetings, are discussed in detail in books such as "The Class Meeting: Reclaiming a Forgotten (and Essential) Small Group Experience" by Kevin M. Watson (Watson, 2013).

of the soul, he thought, is affected by a person's behavior, life choices, and what they project outwardly, is very evident in many people.

It was very fitting for Wesley to ask this specific question.

When we understand the soul, our reason for living comes into focus, and we see life with a new clarity of purpose.

If we truly grasped how deeply our actions shape the state of our souls, how might our behavior change? Imagine a world where we didn't judge people by their appearance, beliefs, or affiliations, but by the true quality of their souls—a world where the essence of a person was visible for all to see.

In [2] Stephen King's *Insomnia*, there's a fascinating take on this idea. The protagonist can see balloons floating above people's heads, each one a different color that reflects the person's true nature. What if we had a similar ability? What if the state of someone's soul was as clear and undeniable as the color of those balloons?

Such a shift would undoubtedly transform how we interact with one another. Would it lead us to treat each other with more compassion, understanding the hidden struggles and strengths within? Or would it present new challenges, forcing us to confront uncomfortable truths about ourselves and those around us?

These questions lie at the core of this exploration. This book aims to dive deep into the essence of our existence as individuals,

---

2. King, Stephen. *Insomnia*. Viking, 1994.

examining the invisible forces that connect our actions to the state of our souls and shaping how we live on this earth. It's an invitation to look beyond the surface and imagine a world where we engage with each other from a place of true understanding and authenticity.

There is precedence across most religious theologies as well as ancient philosophies and mythologies, for the existence of two souls - a mortal soul, sometimes called an "animal soul" or an "earthly soul," associated with the human body, and an immortal soul, sometimes also known as a "free soul," or a "spiritual soul" associated with the spiritual world. Many agree that in order to function correctly, the human body requires both souls to be present at all times.

This concept of various souls or personas responsible for different human behavioral functions has comparisons in modern psychology. The concepts of Id, Ego, and Super-Ego[3] are foundational in the field of psychoanalysis and were developed by Sigmund Freud, the father of psychoanalysis. Freud discusses these ideas in his work [4] "New Introductory Lectures on Psychoanalysis" (Freud S., 1990).

As we delve deeper into the functions of the two souls, this book will explore their distinct roles within the human body.

---

3. The Id represents the instinctual drives of the psyche and operates according to the "pleasure principle," meaning it seeks immediate gratification of all needs, wants, and urges. In other words, it demands immediate satisfaction; when this happens, we experience pleasure. When it's denied, we experience 'unpleasure' or tension.

The Ego is the 'realistic' part that mediates between the desires of the Id and the Super-Ego. It operates on the "reality principle," navigating the tensions of the Id and Super-Ego to maintain a coherent sense of self and reality. The Ego involves reasoning, problem-solving, and other higher mental functions and is responsible for controlling the demands of the Id based on what's socially acceptable. Freud discusses the Ego in depth in "The Ego and the Id" (1923).

The Super-Ego acts as a moral compass or a conscience that interacts with the Id to quell our need for instant gratification and to act in an 'acceptable' way. It represents internalized societal n

4. (Freud S. , 1990) New introductory lectures on psychoanalysis. WW Norton.

The mortal, "animalistic" soul is responsible for driving the body, enabling it to perform daily tasks. It focuses on the physical world, ensuring the body's survival and interaction with its environment.

On the other hand, the immortal "spiritual" soul provides the life-giving spark that keeps the body alive. It also shapes human consciousness and serves a deeper purpose. This immortal soul inhabits the body for a specific reason, one that is crucial to its own journey and key to understanding our *raison d'être*—our true reason for living.

When defining humanity, there are four separate entities that we need to address.

- **The mortal animalistic soul,**

- **The immortal spiritual soul,**

- **The spirit,**

- **The human body.**

As humans, many of us focus a lot on our bodies—how we look, whether we're healthy, or if we're the right weight. It often feels like the body is the most important part of who we are. But for this discussion, the body is really just a tool, like a vehicle, that carries the soul and spirit through life on earth.

From the perspective of the eternal soul, the body itself doesn't hold much importance. Still, it's worth mentioning because understanding both the spiritual and physical sides of being human is key to seeing the bigger picture.

The Animal in Us

To clarify, there are two types of souls: one is mortal, meaning it perishes with the body, and the other is immortal, living on forever. When the body dies, the immortal soul returns to the spiritual realm. (In this book, I refer to "the spiritual realm" without defining it as heaven or attempting to imagine what it might look like from a human perspective.)

Let's start by focusing on the mortal soul. This is the soul that shapes our daily lives. It drives the body and gives it its most basic instincts, influencing how we interact with the world around us.

Figure 1. The attributes of the mortal animalistic soul.

When we are born, or possibly before we are born, we receive a mortal animalistic soul - there is some discussion and disagreements[5] regarding exactly when a soul enters the body, and this is not an argument that I wish to tackle here - for now, we will assume that at some point between conception and birth, a soul enters the body.

The job of the mortal animalistic soul is simple: to keep the body alive. By its very nature, this soul is selfish, as its sole concern is the body's survival and well-being.

For example, think about a baby. A baby can't talk, but it has natural ways of communicating its needs, like crying when it's hungry or uncomfortable, and smiling or cooing when it's happy or content. These instincts are guided by the mortal animalistic soul, ensuring the baby gets the care and attention it needs to survive.

The mortal animalistic soul doesn't stop working once a baby learns to communicate through speech. In fact, its responsibilities increase as the child grows. A toddler, for instance, now has the ability to grab things and take what they feel they need. The actions influenced by the mortal animalistic soul might stay focused on survival, but depending on the environment, they can also evolve into more selfish behaviors.

---

5. Different religions and even different streams within each religion have differing ideas on when the soul enters the human body. This has even become a contentious political topic dictating abortion policy in the United States.

At this stage, children naturally view the world from a self-centered perspective, where everything revolves around their own needs and desires. This self-centrism is another expression of the mortal animalistic soul, ensuring the child gets what they want—whether it's vital for survival or simply something they crave.

It's only around the age of four[6] that children begin to understand that other people have thoughts and perspectives different from their own. This marks the start of their ability to see beyond themselves, a significant shift from the pure self-interest driven by the animalistic soul.

The mortal animalistic soul undeniably takes the lead during the early years of life, and this makes perfect sense. A child relies entirely on this internal force to animate them and ensure their basic needs are met: *I'm hungry; I'm thirsty; I'm uncomfortable; I'm in pain—fix it.* A baby's world is entirely self-focused, as their survival depends on having those immediate needs fulfilled. This self-centeredness is the core purpose of the mortal soul during this stage—to prioritize the "self" and do whatever it takes to keep the new human body alive.

As children grow, however, the natural selfish impulses of the mortal animalistic soul can be tempered through education.

---

6. (Leiden, 2017) Universiteit Leiden. "The importance of relating to others: Why we only learn to understand other people after the age of four." ScienceDaily. www.sciencedaily.com/releases/2017/03/170327083433.htm

Parenting plays a big role in this process, teaching kids to share their toys, be truthful, and interact kindly with others. Beyond basic lessons in behavior, education can also include spiritual or religious teachings that guide children toward greater self-awareness and empathy.

For the sake of understanding how the mortal animalistic soul evolves, let's imagine it left to its own devices—allowed to grow and shape human consciousness as it matures. This perspective helps us explore the unfiltered influence of the mortal soul and how it might develop without the moderating forces of guidance or education.

When a selfish influence like the mortal animalistic soul is allowed to grow unchecked, what does it become? This soul is a force that drives our human consciousness, urging us to meet specific basic needs to survive—sometimes demanding them with urgency. As it develops, the behaviors it influences, especially in children and adolescents, reflect its nature. Common examples include jealousy, aggression toward peers, taking things without permission, greed, lying, and deceit.

In most societies, these behaviors are seen as immature, typical of adolescence, and expected to be corrected over time. However, if left unchecked, these traits can harden into worse characteristics as the person matures, leading to selfishness, narcissism, and extreme egocentric tendencies. The mortal animalistic soul cares solely for the human body, focusing entirely on the "I," the "self," and its needs and desires.

While the mortal animalistic soul plays a necessary role in ensuring survival, it must be guided and restrained. Without control, it can dominate human consciousness, fostering greed, selfishness, and even harmful actions without consideration for others. This unchecked selfishness can spiral into a life consumed by material desires, disregard for others, and impulsive, harmful actions driven purely by personal gain.

The focus of the mortal animalistic soul is always on "me," not "we." It embodies impulsive behavior, greed, and lack of remorse—qualities that align more with animal instincts than the higher virtues we associate with humanity. For example, when someone lashes out impulsively or acts selfishly without remorse, they are often acting under the influence of this soul.

If this strong, unchecked force dominates the human consciousness, it dictates how the body reacts to external stimuli, often in ways that prioritize personal needs above all else. To move beyond this, the influence of the spirit must guide and balance the impulses of the mortal animalistic soul, redirecting its focus toward more selfless and empathetic behavior.

We all know people who seem to embody the characteristics of the mortal soul—selfishness, self-centeredness, and a disregard for others. We encounter them every day: the person who cuts you off on the road, skips the line at the supermarket, or cheats to get ahead. It's easy to label these behaviors as selfish or even thoughtless.

But defining these people as entirely under the influence of their mortal soul—or as inherently "evil"—isn't so simple. The

same individuals might display remarkable kindness and compassion in other situations. They might be the ones who stop to
help a stranger in need or go out of their way to support a friend
or family member.

This is the paradox of the mortal soul. Its influence can bring
out the worst in us in one moment and leave room for profound
acts of care and generosity in another. It reminds us that human
behavior is rarely black and white and that the interplay between
the mortal soul and the spirit creates a complex, dynamic balance in every person.

The Fleeting Breath of Life

So far, we've explored the characteristics of the mortal animalistic soul, which is focused entirely on the "I." Its purpose is
clear: to ensure the initial survival and basic needs of the human
body. It is self-centered by design, driven to protect and sustain
the physical form.

Just as the body relies on the mortal animalistic soul for
survival, it also depends on the immortal spiritual soul—but
the two couldn't be more different. The characteristics and objectives of the immortal spiritual soul stand in stark contrast to
those of the mortal animalistic soul, guiding us toward a higher
purpose beyond mere survival.

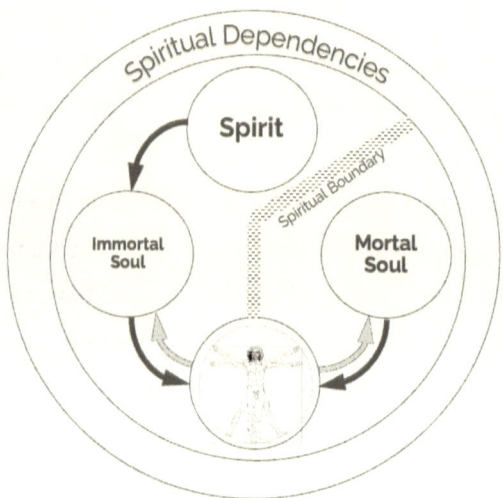

Figure 2. Spiritual Dependencies.

Think of the mortal animalistic soul as the fuel that powers a car. It's essential for keeping the vehicle running. The immortal spiritual soul, on the other hand, is like the spark that ignites that fuel, providing the energy needed to make everything work. Together, they ensure the body functions and stays alive.

At the beginning of life, the immortal spiritual soul is at least a passenger on this journey. It plays a crucial role by providing the spark that animates the body and keeps it moving. This spark is delivered through the spirit, which is contained within the immortal spiritual soul. We'll explore the nature and role of the spirit in more detail later in this chapter.

Figure 3. The attributes of the immortal spiritual soul are influenced by the spirit.

When the immortal spiritual soul enters the human body, it finds itself in an unfamiliar and uncomfortable environment. It's far from its natural spiritual realm, where it's strong, free, and connected to other souls. Within the human body, it's weak, powerless, and unable to influence the body beyond the basic function of keeping it alive—a task it cannot achieve on its own.

For the immortal spiritual soul, being confined in the body feels like a prison. It's cut off from the spiritual community that is its natural habitat, unable to communicate or exert influence. This separation is deeply distressing for the soul, akin to a personal hell. Over time, however, the spiritual soul begins to adapt to its new surroundings. This process is slow and requires significant effort on its part.

During the early years of life, the mortal animalistic soul is in charge, driving the body and focusing solely on survival. The immortal spiritual soul remains subdued, overshadowed by the mortal soul's dominance. Yet, even in these early stages, there are occasional glimpses of the spiritual soul's presence. These moments might show up in small but meaningful ways, like a baby sharing a toy or hugging a loved one—a spark of selflessness breaking through.

As the child grows, the influence of the immortal spiritual soul gradually increases. By the time a toddler begins to develop more awareness of others, the spiritual soul starts to play a larger role, guiding the child toward empathy, kindness, and connection beyond the self.

If the mortal animalistic soul is all about the "I," the immortal spiritual soul is all about the "We." While the mortal soul is focused on selfishly ensuring the body's survival, the immortal soul has no interest in the body itself. Instead, its purpose is to guide the human consciousness toward doing good within the society it inhabits.

These two forces aren't inherently good or evil, although they have the potential to lean in those directions. Rather, they are distinct forces with specific roles at different stages of life. When nurtured and developed properly, they complement each other perfectly.

The mortal animalistic soul ensures the body's physical needs are met, allowing it to survive and function. The immortal spiritual soul, on the other hand, addresses the spiritual needs of the individual, encouraging selflessness, compassion, and a connection to others. Together, they create a balance, enabling a human to thrive both physically and spiritually. Spirituality in this context is what differentiates humans from animals. The more spiritual we are, the more we differentiate ourselves from the animalistic impulses that are associated with the mortal soul.

The concept of balancing different forces or souls within us is not new—it has been a part of human thought for thousands of years. One prominent example comes from Taoism (or Daoism), an ancient tradition of philosophy and religious belief rooted in Chinese culture and worldview. Central to Taoism is the idea of the *Tao*, often translated as "The Way," which represents the sacred, fundamental process of the universe.

A key aspect of Taoist philosophy is the concept of Yin and Yang. These are opposing yet complementary forces that make up everything in the universe. Yin is associated with qualities such as passivity, darkness, femininity, inwardness, and receptivity, while Yang is linked to activity, light, masculinity, outwardness, and initiative.

Taoism teaches that maintaining harmony and balance between Yin and Yang is essential. Their dynamic equilibrium forms the foundation of the Tao. This principle is beautifully represented by the Taijitu symbol, where Yin and Yang swirl together, each containing a small seed of the other. This illus-

trates their interdependence and the ever-changing relationship between the two—a constant reminder that balance is
not static but fluid and dynamic.

This ancient philosophy resonates with the idea of balancing the mortal animalistic soul and the immortal spiritual
soul. Just as Yin and Yang harmonize to create the Tao, these
two souls, with their distinct roles and influences, must work
together to create a balanced and fulfilled human existence.

The immortal spiritual soul starts out in a spiritual realm
where other souls exist. Its purpose is to grow closer to The
Higher Power, to merge with a divine presence. These goals
might seem "selfish" in the sense that the soul wants to
become more spiritual. However, it can't achieve this growth
on its own in its natural environment. It needs an outside
force: the human experience and human consciousness. By
living within a human body, the immortal spiritual soul
encounters the world as The Divine would—experiencing
kindness, compassion, mercy, and other positive qualities
that help it grow spiritually.

Every human is different, guided by free will. Some people fill
their lives with good deeds and positive contributions, helping
the immortal spiritual soul to strengthen and develop. Others
make choices that are harmful and selfish, which can leave the
soul stagnant or even weakened. In this sense, the soul enters

the human body not knowing how it will emerge—improved, unchanged, or diminished.

The immortal spiritual soul's challenge is that it starts off weak inside the human body, which is dominated by the mortal animalistic soul focused on the "I." To fulfill its purpose, the spiritual soul must gradually introduce elements of the "We"—selflessness, empathy, and love—into the person's life. Over time, small shifts in behavior can lead to spiritual growth.

At the end of a person's life, the immortal spiritual soul returns to the spiritual realm. Depending on the experiences it had, it might go back stronger, more aligned with The Divine's plan, or it might not have gained much at all. This book will explore how the immortal spiritual soul can be nurtured and enhanced during its time in a human body, and how, through this process, it can contribute to The Divine's ultimate vision for humanity and the earth.

The Spirit

So far, we've explored the roles of the mortal animalistic soul and the immortal spiritual soul. However, there's a crucial third component in this dynamic: the spirit. Among its many functions, the spirit is what provides humans with consciousness.

Throughout mythology and religion, the concept of the spirit is often referenced. Yet, many traditions don't distinguish clearly between the spirit and the soul, sometimes even using the terms interchangeably. Here, we define the spirit as a unique divine entity closely tied to the immortal spiritual soul.

In many religious traditions, the spirit is viewed as the eternal, divine essence of a person—the "breath of life" that transcends death. It represents the part of a being that connects with The Divine and endures beyond the physical body. In philosophical systems, the spirit is often seen as the conscious self or mind, distinct from the body.

For example, in Cartesian Dualism[7], René Descartes proposed a clear distinction between the mind (or spirit) and the body. He argued that the mind and body are fundamentally different entities: the mind is non-physical, conscious, and immortal, while the body is physical and mortal. Descartes believed this distinction not only supported the idea of free will but also pointed to the immortality of the soul.

By recognizing the spirit as a distinct element, we gain a fuller understanding of the intricate relationship between the body, the mortal animalistic soul, the immortal spiritual soul, and the divine spark that animates human consciousness. This triad forms the foundation of what it means to be human, bridging the physical and the spiritual realms.

As we discussed earlier, while the spirit is tasked with igniting the spark that keeps the body alive, its role extends far beyond that. The spirit serves as the vital connection between the im-

---

7. (Descartes, 1641) Descartes, René. "Meditations on First Philosophy." 1641.

mortal spiritual soul and The Divine. It is the manifestation of The Divine within the spiritual soul—and, by extension, within the human body. Through the spirit, humans carry the "image of God," which is better understood as the positive attributes of The Divine, such as kindness, compassion, and the capacity for selflessness. It is also the spirit that grants humanity consciousness.

It's important to note that being spiritual doesn't require being religious. The defining difference between humans and animals is not the mortal animalistic soul—after all, all living beings possess one. What sets humans apart is the presence of the spirit. By embracing the attributes of the spirit in our actions and choices, we distinguish ourselves from animals and embody spirituality.

> *To be spiritual is to elevate the immortal spiritual soul above the mortal animalistic soul in everything we do*

Spirituality is expressed through our ability to control impulses, think before acting, and be considerate of others. It's in recognizing when someone else needs help, prioritizing others' needs over our own, or delaying gratification for a greater purpose. Each of these acts demonstrates our ability to rise above the purely instinctual drives of the mortal animalistic soul.

Put simply, to be spiritual is to elevate the immortal spiritual soul above the mortal animalistic soul in everything we do. This elevation is the essence of what it means to live with purpose, guided by the spirit, and to embody the higher qualities that connect us to The Divine.

Exhibiting spiritual attributes might sound simple, but for many people, it's far from easy. Human impulses—like greed, gluttony, jealousy, or lust—often arise unexpectedly and can be difficult to control. It's our spirituality that helps us manage and subdue these impulses, guiding us to act with intention rather than instinct.

The spirit, often referred to as the divine breath within us, plays a central role in this process. Carried by the immortal spiritual soul, the spirit embodies and promotes divine attributes[8] such as compassion, mercy, kindness, faithfulness, forgiveness, and restraint (being slow to anger). These qualities not only elevate our actions but also connect us to The Divine, allowing us to live in alignment with a higher purpose.

Animalistic impulses stem from the mortal animalistic soul, which is solely focused on fulfilling the perceived needs of the human body. Its primary concern is survival, with no interest in the spiritual growth or experiences promoted by the immortal spiritual soul. Because of its dominance over the human body, the mortal soul often suppresses the spirit and its influence, thereby limiting the promotion of divine spiritual attributes.

---

8. Exodus 34:6-7

If we are searching for a Higher Power, we must realize that it is closer than we think—right within our own spiritual soul.

Throughout a person's lifetime, the immortal spiritual soul resides within the human body alongside the spirit—a part of The Divine itself. This proximity to the spirit offers the immortal spiritual soul a rare and transformative opportunity for spiritual growth, something it could not achieve in its natural, unbound state. This unique binding of the immortal spiritual soul and the spirit within the human body is deeply significant, particularly from a religious perspective.

For those who are religious, the quest to find God is often a lifelong journey. Yet, the profound truth is that God can be found within each of us—right there in our own souls. The spirit represents The Divine's presence, a gift placed within every human being, ready to guide and inspire when we choose to embrace it.

If we are searching for a Higher Power, we must realize that it is closer than we think—right within our own spiritual soul. By recognizing this, we can connect to The Divine and let the Higher Power's spiritual attributes flow through us to improve the world and humanity. The divine qualities of kindness, compassion, love, and mercy are not just ideals; they are tools within us, waiting to be used. When we cut through the fog created by the mortal animalistic soul and its selfish impulses, we discover a direct line of communication with the Divine.

Tragically, many people, even deeply religious ones, go through life unaware of this profound closeness to The Divine. They may seek God externally without ever realizing that God's presence has been within them all along.

When the immortal spiritual soul is nurtured and its influence grows, while the impulses of the mortal animalistic soul are subdued, the spirit begins to shine through. This transformation is visible to others. A person whose spirit shines through their soul radiates warmth and goodness—they are the kind of person whose presence lights up a room. These individuals, often described as "beautiful souls," reflect divine attributes in all they do, embodying love, kindness, and selflessness.

But there is an even higher state of spiritual growth. While becoming a beautiful soul whose spirit shines outward is a worthy goal, the ultimate objective is to reach a state where we can feel and recognize the spiritual souls of others. In this state, we no longer judge people by their physical appearance or outward traits but by the state of their spiritual soul. Beauty, in this sense, is no longer about physicality but about the health and light of the spiritual soul and how much of the spirit shines through it.

This ideal spiritual state, where we truly see and connect with others on a soul level, is what the Higher Power desires for us. It is not an easy goal, but it is one worth striving for. Even if we don't reach that ultimate state, we can still aim to live in a way where the spirit enhances our soul and where we reflect divine attributes in everything we do. By doing so, we not only grow spiritually ourselves but also bring the divine light into the world around us.

Chapter Three

Discovering Spiritual Balance

The relationship between spiritual entities

The previous chapter introduced the foundational yet intricate concepts of the mortal animalistic soul, the immortal spiritual soul, and the spirit. Each of these entities has its own unique attributes and specific roles within the human experience. We've begun to explore how they interact, influencing one another and, ultimately, shaping the personality and character of a human being.

Mortal Animalistic Primary Attributes	Immortal Spiritual Attributes
Selfishness	Selflessness
Focus on the "I"	Focus on the "We"
Jealousy	Compassion
Greed	Charity
Negativity	Positivity
Bias	Inclusivity
Lust	Love
Narcissism	Kindness
Impulsivity / Violence	Restraint
Cruelty	Mercy

Table 1: Comparing the attributes of each soul.

In **Table 1**, we present a side-by-side comparison of the attributes associated with the mortal animalistic soul and the immortal spiritual soul. It's important to understand that exhibiting one or more attributes from either list does not necessarily mean that one soul is dominant over the other. Depending on the situation, we may display attributes from either soul, in varying degrees and at different times.

For most people, the goal is to live a life guided more by spiritual attributes than by mortal ones. However, it's also crucial to recognize that some negative attributes of the mortal soul are more powerful than others and can lead to a chain reaction, spawning additional negative traits. For this reason, avoiding initial negativity is vital to prevent the development of more destructive patterns.

While the mortal animalistic soul starts off as the dominant force in the human body, the ultimate aim is to subdue its impulses and elevate the influence of the immortal spiritual soul. Ideally, these two souls should work in balance, with the immortal soul reaching at least an equilibrium with the mortal soul to counteract its negative tendencies.

However, the immortal spiritual soul cannot achieve this balance or dominance on its own—it needs the support of the spirit. The spirit, often referred to as the "divine breath," infuses the immortal soul with divine spiritual attributes such as compassion, mercy, kindness, faithfulness, forgiveness, and restraint. These positive qualities, reflective of God's nature, are what Genesis 1:26 refers to as being created in "the image of God."

When the immortal spiritual soul is empowered by the spirit, it gains the strength to overcome the dominance of the mortal animalistic soul. This allows human beings to be guided by a positive purpose, enabling their actions and character to reflect divine goodness. The combined influence of the immortal soul and the spirit creates the potential for a truly fulfilling and spiritually enriched life.

The Caged Soul

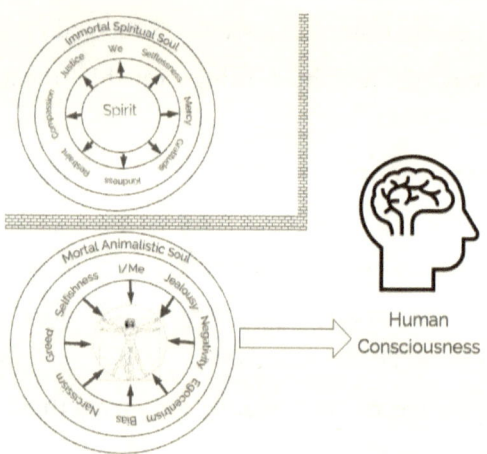

Figure 4: The initial state of the three spiritual entities in the human body.

In **Figure 4**, we observe the initial state of the three entities within the human body. At this stage, the mortal animalistic soul is dominant, with its attributes—or the potential for these attributes—emanating directly from the human consciousness. Its influence drives behavior and decision-making, focusing primarily on the survival and self-centered needs of the individual.

In contrast, the immortal spiritual soul is initially restrained, walled off by a spiritual boundary that limits its ability to promote its positive, divine attributes. It remains in the background, unable to exert significant influence over the human consciousness in this state.

At the core of the immortal spiritual soul lies the spirit, the divine essence imbued with attributes such as compassion, mercy, kindness, faithfulness, forgiveness, and restraint. Although the spirit actively influences the immortal spiritual soul, its impact is not yet strong enough to break through the dominance of the mortal animalistic soul in this early state. This dynamic highlights the initial imbalance between these entities and sets the stage for the struggle to elevate the immortal spiritual soul and the spirit's influence over time.

Figure 5: The Immortal soul infused with the divine attributes.

The immortal spiritual soul reflects the attributes of the spirit, acting as a mirror to project these divine qualities outward. This projection allows the human consciousness to absorb and embody the spirit's attributes, such as compassion, kindness, mercy, forgiveness, and restraint.

The spirit empowers the immortal spiritual soul, giving it the strength and ability to counteract and subdue the dominance of the mortal animalistic soul. Through this process, the immortal spiritual soul becomes a conduit for divine influence, gradually shifting the human consciousness away from the self-centered impulses of the mortal soul and toward a more spiritually aligned and purposeful way of being.

Soul Equilibrium

As we go through life, many of us strive for a state of equilibrium where the mortal animalistic soul and the immortal spiritual soul are in balance. This balance represents an ideal—a harmony between our physical needs and spiritual aspirations. However, life's events and circumstances often disrupt this balance, causing shifts in soul dominance. Many people spend years struggling to overcome selfish desires and impulses, searching for this balance in order to experience a sense of peace and fulfillment. This ongoing struggle is central to the human condition: the fight to become our "best" or most "perfect" selves, even if the goal sometimes feels out of reach.

If the immortal spiritual soul, infused with divine attributes by the spirit, can influence human consciousness and subdue, to some extent, the selfish impulses of the mortal animalistic soul, then a well-balanced life becomes achievable. In such a life, the mortal animalistic soul might still dominate at times, leading to moments of selfishness or ego-centric behavior. Conversely, the immortal spiritual soul might take the lead, fostering positivity, selflessness, and a compassionate outlook.

In this balanced state, a person is not immune to being pulled in one direction or the other. The mortal animalistic soul might assert itself in moments of temptation or stress, while the immortal spiritual soul might inspire acts of kindness, forgiveness, or love. This delicate push and pull between the two souls creates the dynamic tension that defines the human experience. Achieving and maintaining this equilibrium is a challenge, but it is also what makes personal growth and spiritual fulfillment so meaningful.

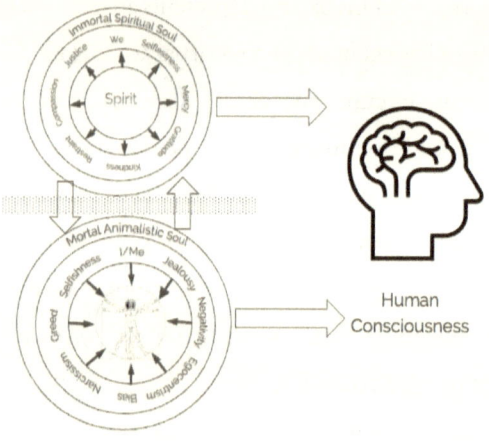

Figure 6: Souls in a state of equilibrium

The state of equilibrium between the mortal animalistic soul and the immortal spiritual soul is what most people experience throughout their lives. In this state, a person may be drawn toward good or evil, depending on external influences and internal struggles. For many, this equilibrium can feel precarious, especially in today's world, which is filled with constant stimuli, materialism, and an unending stream of updates from social media and news outlets. These influences often create feelings of inadequacy, stress, and helplessness, easily disrupting the delicate balance between the souls.

The Dangers of Soul Equilibrium

Living in a state of soul equilibrium in such a fast-paced, high-pressure world can be particularly challenging, especially for adolescents. During this phase of life, young people are still developing the tools to cope with life's stresses, leaving them especially vulnerable to being pulled in multiple directions by external stimuli. Teens are often highly impressionable and can be easily influenced either positively or negatively.

The pressure to maintain balance in this state of flux often drives people—especially adolescents—to seek counseling or mental health support. Many turn to these resources in their search for meaning and stability in their lives. Adolescence is a critical period of self-discovery, during which young people grapple with identity and self-concept. Issues related to self-esteem, body image, and sexual or gender identity often emerge during this time. Moreover, depression and anxiety are among the most common mental health challenges faced by adolescents, manifesting as sadness, loss of interest, fear, or nervousness.

Building a Strong Foundation

When we focus on nurturing the immortal spiritual soul and encouraging its dominance over the mortal animalistic soul, we provide adolescents with a solid foundation for their personal and spiritual growth. By guiding them toward the divine attributes of kindness, compassion, and selflessness, we help them develop a resilient inner compass that can withstand the pull of negative influences. This process not only equips them to navigate the challenges of adolescence but also lays the groundwork for a more balanced, fulfilling, and purpose-driven life.

Spiritual Dominance

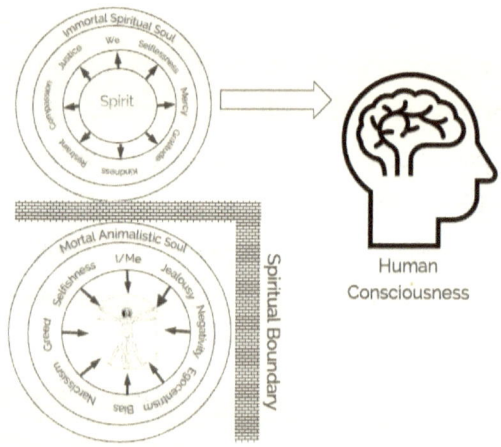

Figure 7: The ideal state of immortal soul dominance

In **Figure 7**, we see the ultimate ideal state: the immortal spiritual soul has achieved dominance over human consciousness, while the mortal animalistic soul is relegated to its original role—performing the basic tasks necessary to sustain the human body. In this state, the immortal spiritual soul fully governs our actions and thoughts, reflecting divine attributes and fostering spiritual growth. Achieving this high level of spirituality brings us closer to the elevated state God desires for humanity.

> *Spiritual growth is a gradual process that requires careful and deliberate steps.*

However, for most of us, reaching this "ideal state" of maximum spiritual dominance is not a realistic goal in our lifetime. Spiritual growth is a gradual process that requires careful and deliberate steps. Attempting to increase spiritual dominance too quickly can have negative repercussions on the human body and psyche. A rushed approach can lead to imbalance, strain, or burnout, undermining the very progress we aim to achieve.

Spiritual development is best approached as a lifelong journey. Each small step strengthens the influence of the immortal spiritual soul, aligns us closer with divine attributes, and helps us create a more harmonious balance within ourselves. By moving forward thoughtfully and patiently, we can grow spiritually while maintaining the stability and well-being needed for a fulfilling life.

Chapter Four

The Religious Soul

If a man reaches the heart of his own religion, he has reached the heart of the others, too. There is only one God, and there are many paths to him. - Mahatma Gandhi

Whether in Jewish ultra-Orthodox sects or various Christian denominations, religion often influences the choice of life partners. While this can create strong bonds within shared traditions, it also places limits on our experiences. By restricting ourselves to those who look, think, or believe like us, we lose the opportunity to engage with and contribute to the incredible diversity of human existence, enriched by a wide array of cultures, ideas, philosophies, and traditions.

Does the Higher Power truly intend for us to divide into social, political, and religious factions that so often lead to conflict, violence, and hatred? Or does the divine vision call for unity and understanding that rises above these divisions?

To begin to understand the Higher Power's hopes for humanity, we must change our perspective. By seeing the world through the eyes of our spiritual soul—our direct connection to the Higher Power—we can look beyond superficial differences and recognize the shared essence of humanity. This divine perspective helps us grasp a vision of love, unity, and mutual growth that transcends boundaries and brings us closer to fulfilling the Divine's ultimate plan.

From a young age, we learn about biology and the organs in our body as part of our education. The soul, however, is a different story. Learning about the soul often requires attending a religious institution, leaving many people without access to understanding its nature or even its existence. But here's the truth: you don't need to be religious to believe in or connect with your soul, nor do you need religion to understand it.

Discussing the soul and spirit naturally leads to thoughts of God or a Higher Power, but tying the soul exclusively to one religion or belief system can be limiting and self-serving. Claiming that any one religious tradition has a monopoly on understanding the soul diminishes its universal significance. Even suggesting that religion as a whole holds exclusive knowledge of the soul is an oversimplification.

Using the concept of the soul as part of a system of rewards and punishments for adhering to specific beliefs is a distortion of its true nature. The soul is not meant to be a tool for control or division; it is a profound and universal aspect of being human, one that transcends any single religion or doctrine. To appreciate the soul in its purest form, we must approach it with openness, free from the confines of dogma or narrow interpretation.

Faith, the bridge between the known and unknown

Faith is an all-encompassing concept that touches many parts of life—religious, spiritual, and even everyday things. It helps shape what we believe, how we connect with others, and how we see the world. Faith can give us meaning, direction, and unity, acting as a guiding light when life gets hard or uncertain.

In religion, faith often means trusting in a higher power, divine presence, or sacred principles. It's different from just believing something to be true; faith goes deeper, involving trust and commitment. For example, you might believe in the teachings of a religion, but having faith means you trust those teachings personally and deeply. As Martin Luther King Jr. said, *"Faith is taking the first step even when you don't see the whole staircase."*

This kind of faith is central to many religions, like Christianity, Islam, Judaism, Hinduism, and Buddhism. It often asks us to trust teachings that can't be scientifically proven but feel true on a moral or spiritual level.

Faith is like a bridge be-
tween what we know and
what we don't.

Spiritual faith is similar to religious faith but isn't tied to any one tradition. Instead, it focuses on belief in something greater—like a higher power, universal energy, or a reality beyond the physical world. Spiritual faith often emphasizes personal growth, connection, and self-discovery as important parts of life.

Faith is like a bridge between what we know and what we don't. It helps us trust and find hope as we face life's mysteries. And faith isn't just about religion—it shows up in other areas too. A scientist might have faith in their theories, an engineer in their designs, or an investor in their choices. Faith requires more than blind trust; it needs learning, commitment, and action.

In the same way, it takes faith to believe that we each have a soul and that a divine presence, in the form of the spirit, exists within us. Faith connects us to something greater than ourselves, but accepting this can be a challenge for some people. Still, faith can open the door to a deeper understanding of life and purpose.

I once knew a man who struggled with alcohol addiction. For years, he denied having a problem, hiding behind lies and deceit, especially from his family. Eventually, the consequences of his addiction caught up with him. He couldn't hold down a job, struggled to function in public, and constantly blamed others for his failures. Anyone familiar with addiction will recognize these patterns of denial and deflection.

Finally, he sought help by going to rehab and joining Alcoholics Anonymous (AA). It was a big step in the right direction, but he hit a stumbling block with the second step of AA's twelve-step program:

> *Come to believe that a Power greater than ourselves could restore us to sanity.*

This step requires faith in a higher power. For many, this doesn't have to mean belief in God—it can be any force or principle that helps them accept they're not in control of everything. However, the concept of a higher power was completely foreign to him. He had spent his entire life dealing with problems alone, never reaching out for help or sharing his struggles with others. To him, his issues were personal and private, something he had to manage on his own.

When he first started attending AA meetings, he hadn't yet opened up about his struggles. For him, accepting the idea of a higher power—and learning to trust others—was a completely new and challenging experience. It required a leap of faith, not only in something greater than himself but also in the process of connecting with others and sharing his story.

He struggled deeply with the concept of a higher power. He didn't believe in God, a divine plan, or even the existence of a spirit or soul. His worldview was stark: there was no afterlife, no spiritual realm, just the here and now, leading inevitably to death. In his mind, humans were simply physical matter, returning to the earth as food for worms after they died. For someone with such a perspective, the journey toward faith and recovery was particularly daunting.

This perspective, filled with futility and despair, reflects what Romanian historian Mircea Eliade termed the *"Terror of History"* (Eliade, 1982)[1] . This concept describes the existential dread that comes from perceiving life as meaningless, defined only by the relentless passage of time and the certainty of death. Without belief in a higher power or a greater purpose, he felt stuck in this bleak worldview, unable to envision anything beyond the physical, material existence.

> *"The 'terror of history,' for me, is the feeling experienced by a man who is no longer religious, who therefore has no hope of finding any ultimate meaning in the drama of history, and who must undergo the crimes of history without grasping the meaning of them."*
>
> Mircea Eliade

---

1. Mircea Eliade, Ordeal by Labyrinth: Conversations with Claude-Henri Rocquet

Eliade used the term *"Terror of History"* to describe the sense of futility that arises from the passage of time, with its apparent randomness, disasters, and humanity's inability to find meaning in existence. It feels as though our time on earth is irrelevant—after we die, time will eventually erase any memory of us. Nothing lasts, and this outlook deeply challenges the human desire for a life of meaning and purpose.

This man embodied that bleak worldview. He had no faith in a higher power, no faith in the support of the group or the healing power of sharing, and likely no faith in the ultimate goals of Alcoholics Anonymous. The idea that there could be a plan for humanity or a reason for our existence was completely foreign to him.

Without faith in the principles of AA, he couldn't fully commit to the twelve-step program, and he wasn't able to overcome his addiction to alcohol. Tragically, like so many others in similar circumstances, he lost everything—his family, his job, his home, and ultimately his life. This heartbreaking outcome illustrates the profound importance of finding faith, whether in oneself, a higher power, or the support of a community, as a foundation for transformation and healing.

No matter our life challenges, we must have absolute faith that we have the power to ultimately achieve our goals. Whether that is faith in God, a higher power, or any other end goal, faith is the critical component that will enable us to get to the finish line. When we lose faith in ourselves and in our own abilities, it can lead to depression and other mental health issues. A [2] study by Orth, Robins, and Meier (Orth, 2009) found a significant link between low self-esteem (which could result from losing faith in one's abilities) and higher vulnerability to depression.

> *"If we lose faith in our abilities, we are likely to experience decreased motivation and performance in other areas of our life as well"* [3]
>
> Bandura, 1977

Faith, while not exclusive to religion, is undeniably a cornerstone of many religious traditions, playing a crucial role in their continuation. For example, believers are often instructed to have faith in the existence of God and in divine teachings. Many religions advocate unwavering faith in their specific theological principles, frequently claiming that their framework represents the ultimate truth—sometimes even the only valid path.

---

2. Orth, U., Robins, R. W., & Meier, L. L. (2009). Disentangling the effects of low self-esteem and stressful events on depression: Findings from three longitudinal studies. Journal of Personality and Social Psychology, 97(2), 307–321.

3. Bandura, A. (1977). Self-efficacy: Toward a unifying theory of behavioral change. Psychological Review, 84(2), 191-215.

Exploiting the Soul and the Spirit

The connection between the human spirit and religion is relatively easy to make, given that the soul is intangible. We cannot see, touch, or pinpoint its exact location in the body, which naturally requires a leap of faith to accept its existence.

However, this very mystery surrounding the soul makes it vulnerable to exploitation. It can be used as a tool to enforce adherence to specific religious doctrines or maintain power structures. Without tangible evidence, individuals are unable to conclusively challenge what they are taught and must rely on faith instead. This dynamic places significant power in the hands of those who define and control religious narratives, often shaping beliefs and behaviors in profound ways.

> *I believe that the soul has*
> *no concept of any specific*
> *religious practice.*

The soul, originating from a realm far beyond the limits of human experience, transcends our capacity for comprehension and conventional thought. It exists outside the framework of human constructs, making it impartial to any particular religious or philosophical affiliation, whether Judaism, Christianity, Islam, Buddhism, Hinduism, or any other belief system. Despite what some religious doctrines might suggest, there are no distinctions between Jewish, Christian, or Muslim souls; all souls share the same essence, purpose, and origin.

This perspective may challenge traditional religious views, but it offers an opportunity to shift how we understand faith and spirituality. By viewing existence through the lens of the soul, we can see beyond the external practices of religion to the deeper purpose of faith. Faith is not solely about rituals or doctrines—it is about elevating our spiritual state and striving to connect with the divine spirit.

Religious practices can support this journey, but I propose that the ultimate aspiration of the soul transcends religious boundaries. It seeks to grow spiritually and unite with the divine, which may align with religious goals yet is not confined to them. This broader understanding can help us focus on the shared essence of humanity and the profound purpose of the soul.

The Perversion of the Soul and Spirit

The concept of soul reincarnation[4] suggests that powerful emotions from past lifetimes can leave lasting impressions on

---

4. Many religions, including Judaism, believe that the soul is reincarnated multiple times. In Judaism, this concept known as 'gilgul neshamot' is central to the belief that a soul will be reincarnated as many times as is necessary in order for it to achieve ultimate spirituality.

the soul, often tied to meaningful spiritual experiences. These emotions may manifest as a deep yearning to reconnect with the positive spiritual encounters of previous lives, sometimes through the exploration of various religious paths. The soul's journey of spiritual growth is a profound and multifaceted topic, one that we will explore in greater depth in later chapters.

> *The Divine force transcends religious boundaries and affiliations.*

In the spiritual realm, the origin of all souls, religion holds no authority. Instead, spirituality reigns, along with an intense desire to connect with the divine presence—God. This Divine force transcends religious boundaries and affiliations. It is not confined to any specific religious framework nor does it exclude souls based on the finite beliefs they held during their earthly existence. Rather, it embraces every soul, regardless of the doctrines or convictions of the mortal body it inhabited.

To some, this idea may challenge long-held teachings or personal beliefs. However, when viewed through the lens of the soul, religion often appears less rigid. What may seem absolute from a human perspective can reveal inconsistencies when assessed from the soul's standpoint.

The soul is singularly focused on spiritual advancement and unity with The Divine. It is unconcerned with the specifics of religious rituals or doctrines, prioritizing spiritual growth above all else. This growth is achieved through positive interactions with others, harmony with the environment, and fostering a connection to the creations of The Divine. By nurturing these connections, the soul progresses on its ultimate journey toward unity with the divine presence.

This "God" or "Higher Power" does not impose exclusion based on the finite beliefs held during earthly existence. It embraces each soul, irrespective of the mortal convictions held by the mortal physical body it inhabited.

The soul cares about one goal above all else: growing spiritually and uniting with The Divine. It doesn't matter which religious practices you follow; what counts is the journey of spiritual development. This growth comes from positive, constructive interactions—both with other people and with the world around us—nurturing a harmonious connection with all of creation.

When we think about God and religion, it's clear that God cares about humans being good and virtuous, just as the soul does. From the Divine perspective, there's a bigger picture. To fulfill this larger vision, humans must foster their soul's spirituality. They do this by raising their own spiritual level and making a positive impact on the world.

The ultimate aim is to recreate a state of spiritual harmony—like the biblical Garden of Eden—where God and all living things coexist peacefully on Earth. Too often, people get caught up in religious rituals and traditions, losing sight of the true purpose of religion: to grow spiritually, enhance virtue, and bring about a more harmonious world.

There are countless paths that can guide us to a higher spiritual state. Each path is unique, offering its own meaningful experiences for those who follow it. These experiences matter deeply to humanity and the soul, but from God's perspective, what's important is the ultimate goal—not necessarily the specific route taken to reach it.[5] Religion plays a role here by providing guidance on the details and methods of spiritual practice, helping people find their way.

Many sacred texts offer frameworks and principles to guide us toward the divine. These writings aren't usually wrong; rather, they present different ways of reaching a higher power. People of faith, who believe in a higher power and value good deeds and social justice, follow these various paths. Yet all these routes, whether guided by scripture or shaped by personal discovery, lead to the same place: spiritual growth.

---

5. The Quran, in Surah Al-Baqarah 2:62, mentions that people of various faiths (including Jews, Christians, and Sabians) who believe in God and the Last Day, and do what is right, will have their reward with their Lord. This might be interpreted as the objective (belief in God, doing right) being more important than the specific path (the individual's religious tradition).

The soul is unconcerned with the specifics of religious practice as long as the path it follows ultimately serves to elevate its spirituality.

However, not everyone finds meaning in traditional religious practices. Today, many individuals feel that standard religious institutions don't meet their personal spiritual needs. They may choose a more individualistic path, forging their own relationship with God or another higher power. Spirituality is deeply personal, and a one-size-fits-all approach often falls short. Where established religions sometimes focus heavily on theology and ritual, many seekers yearn for a more direct, personal spiritual connection—one that can't always be found within organized religious frameworks.

The soul is unconcerned with the specifics of religious practice as long as the path it follows ultimately serves to elevate its spirituality. For the soul, the true measure of religion lies in the spiritual growth it inspires. Similarly, God or any higher power focuses not on the rituals but on the outcomes—the good deeds people perform, the positive environments they create, and the lasting impact they leave behind[6] . The Divine is not absent from the details; instead, they are present within our spirits, concerned with the ultimate goal: a spiritual realm where they can coexist harmoniously with the beings they co-created, as partners in the ongoing act of creation. This concept appears in many religious texts, particularly those envisioning the restoration of divine sovereignty and spiritual harmony at the culmination of time.

> *"Do you not know that your bodies are temples of the Holy Spirit, who is in you, whom you have received from God? You are not your own."*
>
> 1 Corinthians 6:19

Many religions, however, adopt both motivational and punitive approaches. They often discuss the soul's fate after death, asking whether it will experience eternal joy in paradise or unending suffering in hell. Some belief systems declare, "Only by adhering to our theology and practices can salvation be secured; otherwise, eternal damnation awaits." While not all religions

---

6. Positive interactions with humanity and God's creations. Mirroring the divine attributes of compassion, mercy, kindness, justice, etc.

include the concept of hell[7], many agree that the soul is accountable for its earthly actions and that its fate is influenced by how closely its behavior aligns with religious teachings.

> *Religion has monopolized the interpretation of the soul, defining its nature, needs, and journey in ways that serve particular theological agendas.*

I agree that our deeds in this life have a profound and lasting impact on the soul, extending beyond physical death. However,

---

7. Buddhists do not believe in hell as a place of eternal torment. Instead, Buddhism teaches about realms of existence, one of which is the "hell" realm. But being reborn in this realm is not eternal; it's a temporary state based on one's karma. Hinduism has a concept of Naraka, similar to Jainism, but it is not an eternal place of damnation. It is a place where a soul may go to experience suffering as a result of karma, after which the soul is reborn into a new life. There's a wide range of beliefs about the afterlife in Judaism, but generally, the focus is more on life here and now rather than the afterlife.

I believe this connection is not exclusive to any one religious doctrine. Some actions resonate deeply in the spiritual realm, shaping the soul's journey, while others—such as concerns over physical health, wealth, social status, or certain religious rituals—are often significant only in the mortal world and do not carry over into the soul's eternal experience.

Unfortunately, religion has at times monopolized the interpretation of the soul, defining its nature, needs, and journey in ways that serve particular theological agendas. These interpretations are often defended with such fervor that people live—and die—for them. In my view, this approach does not align with the nature of God or any higher power. The soul's essence transcends any specific religious dogma.

I do not subscribe to the idea that God condemns souls to eternal suffering in a fiery hell, whether literal or symbolic. The concept of hell as a place of ceaseless torment seems speculative, rooted in human emotions like vengeance rather than the essence of the soul. Such notions often reflect extrapolations of the physical sensations of pain and are shaped more by human desire for retribution than by divine justice.

While religion can provide valuable spiritual guidance, it has sometimes distorted the true nature of the soul through self-serving interpretations. Extreme theological perspectives often claim exclusivity to salvation—asserting that only their path leads to heaven. Christians may believe salvation is found solely through Jesus, Muslims may see faith in Allah and the teachings of Muhammad as the way, and Jews may view adherence to God's word in the Torah as the key. Each religion presents itself as the holder of ultimate truth.

However, no religion holds the authority to determine who enters heaven or hell. These decisions lie beyond the jurisdiction of human doctrines. Instead of clinging to narrow interpretations, we should explore the true essence of humanity and God. Religion can support the soul's growth, but it does not dictate the criteria for spiritual acceptance or exclusion from heaven. Such matters transcend human understanding and lie solely in the realm of the divine.

Chapter Five

'Garden of Eden' State

We cannot despair of humanity, since we ourselves are human beings. - Albert Einstein

The soul is often perceived as an enigmatic, abstract concept, frequently misunderstood and sometimes exploited by religion to instill fear and enforce obedience. To truly grasp the intricacies of the soul, the spirit, and the devine plan for humanity, it is essential to take a step back and revisit the events that shaped the creation of humanity as we know it today. The Bible, particularly the opening chapters of Genesis, serves as the foundational source for our comprehension of humanity, the soul, and The Divine. In this chapter, we endeavor to explore the reasons behind God's creation of humanity and delve into the origins of the dual souls and the spirit that exist within each of us.

Creation of Humans in the Bible

The following is based upon the narrative in Genesis chapters 1 and 2 and is an interpretation of the events listed in those chapters.

The souls came to God and asked Them if they could be like Them. God replied, "Can you create?" The souls responded, "What is it to create?" So, God created the heavens and earth. Then God created Oceans to show them Their grandeur and trees and plants to show them Their beauty. God created animals to populate Their beautiful creation and gave them their own soul. This simple soul allowed the animals to survive on their own. The souls came to God and asked to be like God. "You can't create, you can't be like Us," responded God, "but we can let you experience what we feel, and then maybe you can emulate us."

God created humans and gave them a piece of Their spirit so that the humans may become animated and inherit God's attributes. The souls entered humans and could instantly feel God's love, compassion, mercy, generosity, and gratefulness. The souls were filled with God's positivity, with all the attributes that define God. For the first time, the souls could feel love, compassion, and the warmth of God's holiness. Now, souls could see through God's eyes, and they could see other souls; they could see and wonder at God's beautiful creations. The longer a soul existed in a human, the more they absorbed God's spirit and God's attributes, and the more like God they became. The souls loved their new state of being. Their holiness became evident to each and every soul, and they strove to become more like God in every way.

However, it was not enough; the souls desired to be exactly like God. They wished to create, be independent, and be as spiritual as God – they wished to become God-like in every possible way. So, they took the animal soul that God had created and added it to their soul. The animal soul infected the human body and caged the spiritual soul within the human body. The animal soul instantly took control of the human body, infecting its consciousness with negativity, brutality, and greed. The spiritual soul could no longer experience God's attributes; it could no longer see through the human eyes as God sees. Instead, it could only feel the attributes of the animal soul: attributes of selfishness, greed, and hunger.

God was angry at the souls, yet They took mercy on the souls. "From now onwards, you will leave the spiritual realm and suffer inside a human caged together with the animal soul that you placed there. This will be a punishment and an opportunity to repair the damage you have done by trying to be Us. Your task will be to recreate the state you have destroyed. You will be responsible for influencing humans to shed the attributes of their animal soul and mirror Our attributes so that you may experience Our spirituality again." God gave the souls a piece of Their spirit so that they may always carry God's attributes with them and always know of Their holiness. They then named the ultimate spiritual state that had been destroyed "The Garden of Eden." They ordered souls to recreate the state of the Garden of Eden. From this point onwards, a soul's purpose would be to grow its spirituality by influencing humans to emulate God's attributes and become spiritual by conquering the powerful urges of the animal soul.

Biblical Interpretations

While this story is fictional, it demonstrates the interplay between the mortal soul and the spiritual soul. The Bible can help inform us of how humans acquired two very different souls. What was God's original intention for humans? The following study is revolutionary in its assumptions and in how it looks at the biblical narrative, not from a human's perspective but rather from the perspective of God and the soul itself. For the sake of this discovery, we are interested in what actions God took to create humans as we know them today.

In fact, there were two events that are relative to this narrative:

> *The Lord God formed man from the dust of the earth. He blew into his nostrils the breath of life, and man became a living being.*
>
> Genesis 2:7

Here, it is evident God made a human, but what They created was no more than a model. It was an inanimate object, just as you would form a vase from clay; it can't move, it can't think, it is just a clay vase - it is no more than that. In order to provide this inanimate object with life, God took a piece of Their life-force and breathed it into this model of a human. What They breathed into the human was, in fact, Their spirit; in doing so, They created a perfect spiritual vehicle through which the soul could enjoy God's creation. The spirit is what gave humans the ability to be animated, move, and behave not as animals but as living beings, albeit with very limited capabilities.

In their earliest state, humans were creatures that had no self-awareness; they knew nothing of the world they lived in; they had no desires or objectives other than to be a temporary home for a soul. God crafted human bodies for the souls to inhabit; They created a place akin to heaven on earth. Souls could come and experience God's ability to create; They showed the souls Their wonderful creations on earth. Souls could experience Their divine positive attributes through the medium of a human that was formed in God's image. Souls could marvel at God's creations through a being that represented God in every physical way but without God's divine capabilities of creation. This is what God's intention was initially for humans; the human body was a vehicle for souls to exist temporarily in this world in order that they may experience the world, God's creation, through God's eyes and increase their level of spirituality almost to the point where they would be on God's spiritual level.

We will learn later that the spiritual soul has no concept of the body. It neither cares for the body in life nor in death; it is just a vehicle for the soul that it occupies for a relatively short amount of time. The soul has no physical form that we, as humans, can relate to. It requires the human form in order to interact with the divine creation, but at the same time, it cares nothing for the well-being of this physical form.

The following important episode is found later in Genesis Chapter 3:

> *And the serpent said to the woman, "You are not going to die, but God knows that as soon as you eat of it your **eyes will be opened** and you will **be like divine beings who know good and bad.**" When the woman saw that the tree was good for eating and a delight to the eyes, and that the tree was desirable as a source of wisdom, she took of its fruit and ate. She also gave some to her husband, and he ate. Then the **eyes of both of them were opened and they perceived that they were naked;** and they sewed together fig leaves and made themselves loincloths.*

> Genesis 3:4-7

Until this point, humans existed as passive vessels, carrying out God's will without independent thought or inquiry. They were set apart from the other creatures God had fashioned, for humans contained God's own spirit and were endowed with a distinctly different soul than that of the animals. Whereas animals possessed a mortal soul fixated on basic survival, humans were given a soul originating from the Divine—a purely spiritual entity unconcerned with the physical body's preservation. Instead, its sole focus lay in matters of spirituality. All essential requirements for the body's continued life were supplied by God's own spirit, thereby underscoring the fundamental differences between the mortal animal soul and the immortal spiritual soul bestowed upon humanity.

I believe it was never God's original intention for humans to eat from the metaphorical Tree of Life or the Tree of Knowledge. God had already provided a perfect environment where souls could appreciate creation and grow spiritually. Yet, for reasons likely tied to the soul's deep longing to increase its spirituality, maybe to be "god-like," the souls performed an action God did not anticipate: they ate from the Tree of Life.

The Tree of Life grants life, but not the kind God intended for humans. Instead, it provides the kind of life meant for animals. When a human body, already containing a spiritual soul, is infused with an animalistic soul, unpredictable consequences arise. One might wonder why God placed this source of animal souls within human reach. The reason is that humans, blessed with a spiritual soul, were meant to act on God's behalf as guardians of creation—caring for and managing it. The Tree of Life was there for them to oversee and maintain for the benefit of the animals, but not to consume for themselves. It's as if they were given a deadly potion to safeguard: harmless for its intended recipients but lethal if they tried it themselves.

God entrusted the Earth and all living things to humans, not for abuse, but for stewardship. By caring for God's creation, humans would work alongside God, fulfilling their role as keepers of the world.

The Tree of Life served as the source of animalistic souls. Until this point, humans possessed only a spiritual soul—one that knew only God and spirituality. But when they took from the Tree of Life, they gained a very different kind of soul meant for animals—a soul focused on physical survival. Instead of God's spirit animating their bodies, this new soul took over. Consumed by greed, humans then ate from the Tree of Knowledge, suddenly becoming aware that they had physical bodies.

> "*Then the* **eyes of both of them were opened, and they perceived that they were naked.**"

They suddenly became aware of their bodies. With the animalistic soul and the knowledge it provided, humans could now think for themselves. They were no longer entirely under God's will. They could look after their own needs, decide what seemed good for them, and even question God. This new awareness made them self-focused, introducing feelings like selfishness, jealousy, and vanity, all aimed at protecting and benefiting their own bodies.

By taking in the animalistic soul, another change occurred: the spiritual soul, which had once freely enjoyed God's creation, could no longer guide the human mind. Instead of fulfilling its purpose of experiencing creation through God's perspective and reflecting divine attributes, it became trapped. It had no way to leave the body, no way to influence the human, and no chance to complete its spiritual mission. The spiritual soul, in effect, became a prisoner of the animalistic soul that now controlled the human body and thoughts.

In Genesis Chapter 3, verse 9, God seeks out humans (the souls) but does not find them as He once did. Traditional interpretations say that God, being all-knowing, certainly knew what had happened and where the humans were hiding. However, God asked questions to engage them in conversation rather than immediately punishing them for their disobedience.

> *They heard the sound of the LORD God moving about in the garden at the breezy time of day; and the man and his wife hid from the LORD God among the trees of the garden. The LORD God called out to the man and said to him, "Where are you?" He replied, "I heard the sound of You in the garden, and I was afraid because I was naked, so I hid."*

> Genesis 3:8-10

From the soul's point of view, it's clear that when God asked, "Where are you?" in the Garden of Eden, They were searching for the spiritual soul that once fully inhabited the human form. But God no longer found it in its pure state because that soul was now hidden behind the animal soul that the humans had taken in. All God could sense at that moment was a human mixed with an animalistic soul, not the untainted spiritual soul that once occupied the body alone.

God created the Garden of Eden as a space for spiritual souls to experience the world, to reflect divine qualities, and to grow in holiness. Humans were meant to hold a spiritual soul—part of God's own life force—and live as holy, spiritual beings, mirroring the divine. But the souls disrupted this plan by blending an animal soul into a body that already held a spiritual soul. This brought self-awareness to humans and stripped them of their original purity. Suddenly, humans were no longer fit to dwell in God's spiritual paradise on Earth. Their role changed drastically: they were no longer simply vessels allowing the spiritual soul to fully experience the divine creation through God's perspective. Instead, they became a mix of spiritual and animalistic drives, preventing the soul from freely imitating divine attributes.

With the spiritual soul now obscured by the animal soul, God's initial plan for humanity could no longer proceed as intended. The introduction of two souls in one body fundamentally altered the human experience, forcing God's plans for humanity and the soul's journey to change in response to this new reality.

Humans had become intelligent and independent. They could think for themselves, provide for their own needs, experience a wide range of emotions, and even create things—traits that made them almost like the divine. I say "almost" because there was one key difference: God could create something out of nothing, as seen in the creation of the universe, while humans could only create using materials that already existed.

Living in a 'Garden of Eden' State

A Midrash[1] tells us that before God sent Adam and Eve out of the Garden of Eden, God showed them how to make fire by striking two stones together. From that point on, humans were free to create on their own, yet always with the knowledge passed down from God. No matter what they achieved, humans would never produce something truly from nothing as God once had.

> *The Garden of Eden is a state of very high spirituality where we embrace the Divine qualities and*

---

1. Genesis Rabbah 11:1

view the universe as God
does.

When we look closely at the first two chapters of Genesis, it becomes clear that the Garden of Eden wasn't just a physical place, but rather a very special state. This state existed only as long as humans had a spiritual soul that could experience creation and understand God's attributes directly, as if seeing the world through God's own eyes.

I call this state the "State of the Garden of Eden." It's a high spiritual condition in which we fully embrace God's positive qualities and view the world almost as God does. In this state, we stop judging people by their physical appearance. In fact, we don't even see the body's outward features as important anymore—just a temporary vessel for the spiritual soul. This is what God originally intended when creating the Garden of Eden: a place where souls could be appreciated for their spiritual nature rather than their physical form.

However, once humanity absorbed the animalistic soul, their spiritual vision became blocked. Humans can no longer enjoy that high spiritual state because the spiritual soul is now trapped and overshadowed by the animalistic soul. Regaining this "State of the Garden of Eden" isn't impossible, but it's challenging. It requires effort, self-improvement, and spiritual work. This, I believe, is what God now wants from us.

When humans first became self-aware, the original state of the Garden of Eden could no longer exist. Our task now is to strive toward that state again, to lift ourselves above mere physical concerns and see each other's souls as God intended.

The Divine could have chosen to destroy this human creation, something They never planned to allow in the first place. Yet, instead of wiping it out entirely (as we later see God consider doing in the story of Noah[2]), They allowed humans with their two souls to continue existing. From that moment on, humans had lost the original purity of their spiritual vision and were guided by their animal instincts as well.

Still, God wanted humans to live on a level above the animals. To make this possible, humans needed both the spiritual soul and the animalistic soul. The spiritual soul was needed to lift them above a purely animal existence, but the animalistic soul was needed for survival in the physical world. Both souls had to remain in the human body for life to continue. Yet this meant the spiritual soul's role changed dramatically—it could no longer see the world through God's perspective. Humans now saw only through human eyes, not divine ones. It's like how a deaf person can't fully appreciate the brilliance of Mozart or Bach as someone who can hear.

From this point forward, the spiritual soul was forced to leave its spiritual home and endure the challenge of living inside a human body, trapped alongside the mortal animalistic soul. Instead of simply viewing the world as God does, the spiritual soul had to grow and improve itself from within this limited,

---

2. Genesis 6:11–9:19

physical existence. Humans became partners with God in trying to fix what had been broken. Each positive act by humans would strengthen and enrich the spiritual soul, helping to rebuild what their earlier actions had destroyed.

In a sense, it's poetic justice: after altering God's original plan, the spiritual souls now had to live within their own creation, working hard to repair what they themselves had damaged. This is the human condition as we know it today—humans living with both an animalistic soul and a spiritual soul, striving to restore what was lost and become the caretakers of creation that they were always meant to be.

Chapter Six

The Origins of Evil

The battle line between good and evil runs through the heart of every man. - Aleksandr Solzhenitsyn

Understanding Soul Functions

Evil is an inherently complex concept that experts in psychology, sociology, criminology, philosophy, and religion continually strive to define and understand. Some view evil merely as the absence of goodness, while others interpret it as the deliberate infliction of harm intended to undermine societal well-being. Religious traditions often offer their own explanations for the origins of evil and its manifestations in human behavior. As a result, evil can emerge in numerous forms and stem from a variety of underlying motives.

In the upcoming discussion, we will explore how evil might begin to surface by examining the interplay among three key components of human existence: the mortal animalistic soul,

the immortal spiritual soul, and the spirit. To comprehend
how the mortal soul could give rise to hatred, we must first
understand the roles each soul plays, along with how they
collectively shape our thoughts, choices, and actions.

As established in Chapter 2, the immortal spiritual soul
enters the human body at a distinct disadvantage. At birth,
the mortal animalistic soul takes precedence, holding sway
over our consciousness and primarily attending to immediate physical survival needs. At this early developmental
stage, the mortal soul cannot be deemed evil. Its priorities
revolve around ensuring that the newborn remains alive,
secure, and well-cared-for. Thus, what might be seen as
self-centeredness at this point is nothing more than a survival mechanism, vital for the infant's continued existence.
Over time, however, as the human consciousness matures
and the interplay of souls evolves, the conditions that allow
for more harmful tendencies—such as hatred—may gradually take shape.

From what we have established so far, the mortal animalistic soul primarily ensures the newborn's physical survival. At
this early stage, its influence naturally dominates because it is
perfectly suited for attending to the infant's immediate needs:
nourishment, protection from harm, and basic comfort. In
contrast, the immortal spiritual soul remains largely dormant
during these initial years, precisely because it originates from
a realm devoid of physical requirements. It lacks any intrinsic
understanding of the human body's needs, such as clothing,

shelter, or sustenance, and thus cannot initially contribute to the body's preservation.

This dichotomy is illustrated in the biblical narrative of Adam and Eve (Genesis 3:4–7), who only became aware of their nakedness—and by extension, their physical state—after they had eaten from the Tree of Knowledge. Prior to that moment, they existed in a condition akin to that of the immortal spiritual soul, indifferent and unresponsive to basic human concerns. Only with the influence of the mortal soul did they recognize their bodily vulnerability and the consequent need for clothing and other protective measures.

Both souls possess distinct roles: the mortal animalistic soul ensures the body's immediate well-being and survival, while the immortal spiritual soul focuses on fostering spiritual growth and higher principles. Over time, however, either soul can ascend to a position of dominance. The mortal animalistic soul, having held sway since birth, finds it easier to maintain control, often emphasizing self-preservation and material concerns. In contrast, the immortal spiritual soul must exert significant effort to assert itself within the human consciousness. Should it become dominant, it may lead to unexpected results for the body, as it remains fundamentally unconcerned with physical survival. On the other hand, unbridled dominance of the mortal soul can prove equally destructive, though its destruction often stems from an overzealous commitment to self-preservation and material gain.

The critical distinction lies in their underlying priorities. The mortal animalistic soul will go to great lengths—even extreme measures—to protect the body, whereas the immortal spiritual soul does not regard the body as inherently important and can detach from it without a sense of loss. Understanding this profound difference offers valuable insight into how both benevolent and malevolent tendencies can emerge within human beings. Each soul fulfills a predetermined purpose—the mortal soul for physical sustenance, the spiritual soul for moral and spiritual elevation—and each assumes its respective significance at different stages of human life.

The Roots of Evil

When a baby is born, its body isn't filled with evil or hatred. Instead, you can think of the newborn's body as a blank container that will eventually hold the immortal spiritual soul. At the start, the mortal animalistic soul takes charge, focusing on one thing: making sure the body survives. At this early stage, that self-centered approach isn't evil—it's just practical. It ensures the baby gets fed, kept clean, given company, and protected, providing a sense of safety and happiness. These are all normal and essential needs for a newborn.

However, as the child grows, their needs become more complex. Over time, if the mortal soul's self-centered tendencies aren't guided or balanced, the child can become more demanding, entitled, and focused only on their own desires. This can show up in behaviors like bullying, taking things that aren't theirs, or even using violence. Unfortunately, these problems often start in early childhood, and many times adults don't address them properly.

> *The human body does*
> *not come into the world*
> *tainted with evil or hate.*

In some societies, selfishness is even encouraged. Rabbi Adin Steinsaltz, in his book *The Soul* (2018), notes that certain cultures—like ancient Sparta or some wealthy social circles—view selfishness and self-interest as strengths. Even in modern Western societies, some parents raise their children to feel overly special and deserving of everything, which can lead to selfish or entitled behavior. They teach children that if they don't grab what they want, someone else will take it. This mindset reinforces an "it's all about me" attitude.

When kids grow up believing they are the center of the universe, they often develop traits like egocentrism, narcissism, and a lack of empathy. If no one intervenes, these traits can cause serious problems later in life, making it hard for them to form healthy relationships. Such individuals might expect special treatment, can't handle criticism, and don't think about other people's feelings. Still, it's important to note that not everyone who is entitled or selfish turns into someone with a severe personality disorder, like a sociopath or a psychopath. Those conditions usually stem from a mix of genetics, brain factors, and harmful childhood experiences, not just from growing up entitled.

Raising a child to be overly selfish and entitled puts them at a spiritual disadvantage. This means they are leaning heavily towards the mortal animalistic soul, which focuses only on "me, me, me," rather than balancing it with the immortal spiritual soul, which encourages empathy, kindness, and spiritual growth. Parents might teach selfishness and entitlement because of their own beliefs, fears, or cultural norms. They might think this is how to help their kids succeed or survive in a tough world.

Lastly, it's worth remembering that not all forms of self-focus are bad. A healthy amount of self-interest can be good—it helps with self-care and staying safe. The key is to find a balance. As a child grows, helping them develop a mix of caring for themselves and caring for others leads to more stable, positive relationships and a better-adjusted personality overall.

Evil and hate aren't part of our natural makeup; they're learned behaviors that develop over time. Throughout history, people have argued about whether humans are born good, bad, or completely neutral. In my view, before a young child fully understands the world or can copy their parents' behaviors, they aren't inclined toward either good or evil. It's up to parents to introduce the idea of right and wrong. Our mortal animalistic soul gives us a starting point: survival instincts that appear as selfishness. If parents teach a child to hate, that hate takes root in these selfish tendencies. The child isn't born with hate; it's planted and allowed to grow in the fertile soil of the mortal soul's self-interest.

> *The impulses that corrupt: sex, greed, and power—are closely tied to the mortal animalistic soul.*

People who show signs of selfishness, entitlement, or egocentrism are usually driven by their mortal animalistic soul. Because of this, they naturally seek out others who think the same way. This pattern appears in many areas of life, but it's especially clear in politics. We've all seen politicians who put their own needs first, willing to sacrifice the well-being of an entire nation to feed their egos or hold onto their power. Even those who start out wanting to help others often lose their original ideals as they get a taste of power. The impulses that corrupt—sex, greed, and power—are closely tied to the mortal animalistic soul. Once a politician gains power, they may crave more, often showing less empathy toward the people affected by their actions. This decline in empathy, a quality linked to the immortal spiritual soul, can have serious, harmful consequences for the public.

Greed for Money

In a capitalist society, financial resources are indispensable for ensuring one's survival and maintaining a basic standard of living. The mortal animalistic soul, inherently focused on safe-guarding the human body's well-being, thus perceives material wealth as critically important. While a great many individuals remain satisfied with their allotted portion, others are driven by an insatiable appetite for material gain. The biblical verse from Proverbs 30:8 offers insight into this delicate balance:

> *"Keep lies and false words far from me; Give me neither poverty nor riches, but provide me with my daily bread."*[1]

Proverbs 30:8

This verse underscores the hazards at both ends of the eco-nomic spectrum. On the one hand, dire poverty may compel a person to engage in desperate measures simply to survive, eroding moral boundaries in the process. On the other hand,

---

1. Translation by jps.org.

unfettered wealth can give rise to hubris, selfishness, and an ever-increasing hunger for more, ultimately distorting one's moral compass. The wisdom found in Proverbs encourages a principle of moderation—recognizing that both deprivation and excess can be spiritually, morally, and emotionally perilous.

The desire for wealth, when left unchecked, can lead individuals down a treacherous path. Some may resort to outright criminality—stealing, embezzling, or engaging in fraudulent schemes—to amass riches. Even those who refrain from illegal activities might find themselves perpetually unsatisfied, constantly craving greater amounts of money. Such unbounded ambition often damages personal relationships and fractures family bonds. Inheritance disputes offer a clear example, where siblings and relatives turn against one another, initiating legal battles fueled by greed. Significantly, this phenomenon transcends cultural and religious boundaries—unbridled avarice manifests in all societies, irrespective of professed moral principles.

It is not uncommon for adherents of religious traditions that emphasize love, charity, and moral fortitude to become entangled in the pursuit of wealth. Christianity, for instance, advocates compassion and benevolence toward others, while Judaism highlights the importance of honesty, altruism, and aiding the less fortunate. Nevertheless, these religious imperatives can be overshadowed by the mortal animalistic soul's drive for acquisition. Such instances illuminate the formidable power of the mortal soul's influence, even in the face of deeply held spiritual convictions.

If the mortal animalistic soul dominates one's consciousness without meaningful restraint or counterbalance, it can precipitate profound personality distortions. Individuals holding influential positions may succumb to egocentrism, greed, and narcissism—traits frequently misconstrued as inherently evil or demonic. Yet these tendencies are better understood as the mortal soul's survival-driven impulses operating without moral guidance or spiritual oversight.

In contrast, when the mortal soul's impulses are tempered by the presence of the immortal spiritual soul—infusing a person's character with empathy, virtue, and a sense of higher purpose—a more balanced and ethically sound individual emerges. This synergy between the two souls fosters a state of equilibrium, in which self-interest is counterbalanced by compassion and moral reasoning. Such harmony stands at the core of what we might term a "normal" or well-adjusted human being, capable of engaging with the world in a just and spiritually coherent manner.

The Soul, Torture, Murder, and Divine Influence

The Bible presents us with a perplexing paradox. On one hand, God expressly forbids taking a human life, as stated in the Ten Commandments:

"You shall not murder."
Exodus 20:2–17 and Deuteronomy 5:6–21

This directive would seem to apply universally. Yet, not long before this commandment is pronounced, the same God instructs the Israelites to completely annihilate the Amalekites. Furthermore, additional scriptural accounts record God commanding the Israelites to wage war against other nations:

- In **Numbers 31**, God instructs Moses to engage in warfare against the Midianites as retribution for their role in leading the Israelites away from God's path.

- In the **Book of Joshua**, the Israelites are commanded to conquer the land of Canaan. This includes the iconic episode at Jericho (Joshua 6:1–21), where they march around the city walls for seven days before God miraculously brings the walls down, enabling the Israelites to overrun the city.

- In **1 Samuel (15:1–3)**, God commands King Saul to obliterate the Amalekites in response to their earlier enmity.

- In the **Books of Samuel**, King David consults God regarding various military campaigns and follows divine guidance to defeat Israel's adversaries, notably the Philistines.

Commentators throughout history have grappled with reconciling this apparent contradiction. One widely accepted approach focuses on the translation of the Hebrew term rendered as "kill" in the commandment "Thou shall not kill." Many modern Christian translations clarify this as "You shall not murder," a distinction crucial in English. "Murder" implies a deliberate, unlawful, and morally unjustified act of taking a life. Conversely, "killing" is a broader term and may, under certain circumstances—self-defense, warfare, or sanctioned legal processes—be deemed permissible or even necessary. While modern societies continue to debate the morality of capital punishment or warfare, from the biblical perspective, the wars waged under divine command were seen as orchestrated punishments against nations deemed wicked. Thus, while murder (the malicious and unjustified taking of a life) remains unequivocally forbidden, not all acts of killing are equally condemned in the biblical narrative.

This leads us to a more profound and enduring question: **Where is God when murder occurs, and can such tragedies be prevented?** This inquiry delves into the realm of theodicy, derived from the Greek words for "God" and "judgment." Theodicy wrestles with the paradox of a deity who is simultaneously all-loving, all-knowing, and all-powerful, yet allows evil to persist. Why does an omnipotent and omnibenevolent God tolerate hatred, cruelty, and especially the suffering of innocents?

Where is God when murder occurs, and can such tragedies be prevented?

As we have determined, violence correlates strongly with the mortal animalistic soul, which embodies primal instincts centered on survival and self-interest. Harming another human being on a whim, without moral restraint, reflects the height of animalistic brutality and the absence of spiritual refinement. Since the dawn of human history—evident in the narrative of Cain and Abel—humans have demonstrated the capacity to inflict appalling cruelty upon one another. Whether a solitary murderer or a genocidal regime, the fundamental nature of the act remains the same: an unjustified taking of human life.

Consider large-scale atrocities such as the Holocaust. During these cataclysmic events, it appears that God remains silent or inert, unable or unwilling to intervene to halt the killings. In his memoir *Night*, Elie Wiesel articulates this sensation of abandonment, lamenting the seeming absence of divine intervention amid unimaginable suffering. Could it be that God is simply unaware, indifferent, or powerless against these acts of evil?

To reconcile this unsettling notion, we return to the relationship between God, the mortal animalistic soul, and the immortal spiritual soul. The divine spark resides within the immortal soul as the spirit. This spirit, linked to the divine, is not concerned with the physical body's survival nor does it involve itself directly in the mortal soul's impulses. The mortal animalistic soul, preoccupied with self-interest and capable of harboring hatred, may commit murder without encountering intervention from the spirit—or by extension, from God. In other words, it appears God has deliberately limited divine influence to preserve human free will. Humanity, created in God's image, possesses moral agency, the capacity to choose between right and wrong. God's decision to respect human freedom places a boundary on divine interference.

> *God has deliberately limited divine influence to preserve human free will.*

This does not imply that God never intervenes in human history. There are instances where God appears to shape large-scale outcomes, such as the eventual collapse of the Nazi regime, thereby ending the Holocaust. Yet, at the individual level, God refrains from overriding personal free will, even when individuals choose evil. Thus, divine commandments, including the prohibition of murder, serve as moral guidelines intended to prevent humans from committing atrocities. However, God relinquishes direct control over individual moral choices. Human beings are free to obey or defy divine moral law.

In essence, this perspective suggests that God, while fully capable of influencing the broader currents of history, exercises restraint in personal matters of right and wrong. Divine providence may guide or create circumstances for the ultimate downfall of evil systems, but the immediate moral decisions—such as whether to kill—remain the domain of the mortal animalistic soul and human free will. This delicate interplay attempts to resolve the tension between divine goodness, human agency, and the persistent presence of evil in the world.

Sarah, now a devout Christian, recounts a story from when she was fourteen years old.

> "When I was fourteen, I liked to hang out with older girls. I think that they were about two years older than me, but I really looked up to them as role models. Once, we were hanging out after school when a pickup truck stopped near us. A couple of guys got out and asked if we wanted to go to a party. The older girls, who knew the guys, agreed to go with them, and I went along as well. It turned out to be a bachelor party, and during the party, I was forcibly rapped by one of the guys. Later, I asked God why this happened to me and why He didn't stop it. God responded to me very clearly in a dream that same night. He told me that He wanted to stop them. He tried to convince the boy to stop rapping me. He tried with all his might to trigger the boy's

consciousness, but it was to no avail. His earthly soul was too powerful."

This narrative suggests that while God is aware of everything happening in the world, divine influence might be limited to those individuals who have already established a connection with their spiritual souls. By granting humanity free will, it appears that God chose to place boundaries on the ability to directly influence the mortal animalistic soul and, as a result, human behavior. This idea represents a foundational and potentially transformative way of understanding the relationship between the divine and humanity.

The concepts introduced here are undoubtedly controversial, and it's entirely understandable that many would disagree with them. My goal has been to approach the mystery of extreme human violence from the perspective of the souls, an angle that is admittedly both challenging and unconventional. I acknowledge that this short exploration likely only scratches the surface of a deeply complex issue. Still, I hope that the fundamental ideas presented can serve as a starting point—one that might be expanded and examined more thoroughly in future discussions or writings.

Chapter Seven

Cultivating the Spiritual Soul

We are not human beings having a spiritual experience. We are spiritual beings having a human experience. - Pierre Teilhard de Chardin

In Chapter 3, we learned that the spirit influences the immortal soul and therefore inherits its divine attributes. At a glance, it may appear that the more prominent the immortal spiritual soul becomes, the more spiritual we turn out to be, leading us towards performing virtuous deeds. However, this assumption is not entirely correct. The spirit, which is a part of the immortal soul, is not something the human consciousness can fully grasp, as it represents a sliver of the divine Higher Power. If we attain a high spiritual state where the immortal spiritual soul governs our human consciousness, we simultaneously open our physical form to the spirit, a phenomenon that our brain may struggle to comprehend or accommodate. For some individuals, exposure to the spirit at this intensity can result in borderline personality disorders, psychosis, and numerous other personality disorders. Therefore, it is crucial to incrementally and cautiously nurture the dominance of the immortal soul.

A longstanding tradition in Judaism discourages the study of the Kabbalah[1] before the age of 40 or before the student has mastered all other texts and demonstrated evident spirituality and scholarship. The sages opined that exploring the universe's mysteries and exposure to The Divine could result in students becoming detached from this world, hinting that their brains might be unable to assimilate and fathom the spiritual essence of The Divine. There are numerous documented instances in modern times where individuals have shown signs of psychosis or psychotic-like symptoms after intensive interaction with religious texts or concepts. However, one must remember that correlation does not necessarily equate to causation. The manifestation of psychotic symptoms usually involves a variety of factors, including individual predisposition, environmental stressors, and other personal circumstances.

---

1. Kabbalah is a form of Jewish mysticism that interprets the Bible in an esoteric manner. Kabbalah seeks to define the nature of the universe and the human being, the nature and purpose of existence, and various other ontological questions.

For example, the Jerusalem Syndrome[2] (Bar-El, 2000) refers to the phenomenon where individuals develop profound religious delusions or hallucinations after a visit to the city of Jerusalem, often centered around biblical figures or concepts.

Similarly, a recognized condition called "religious delusion"[3] (Siddle, 2002) exists, where a person's beliefs become dissociated from reality in the context of their religious faith. This condition can occur as part of broader psychiatric conditions like schizophrenia, bipolar disorder, or other forms of psychosis.

As the immortal soul attempts to assert its dominance in human consciousness, it's essential not to rush this process, bypassing necessary steps to condition the human brain to the divine spirit. Not everyone will achieve an elevated level of spirituality, and it is sufficient for most people to have a dominant spiritual soul influencing their consciousness with divine qualities.

The Immortal Soul and the Physical Form

The immortal spiritual soul serves as a vital counterbalance to the mortal animalistic soul's self-centered inclinations, elevating our spiritual consciousness. Yet, when the immortal soul gains ascendancy within a person's mental framework, it can have complex and sometimes detrimental effects on the physical body. Previously, we discussed how heightened spiritual states might give rise to certain mental conditions. Here, we turn our attention to the direct physical repercussions of a strong spiritual focus.

The mortal animalistic soul is intimately bound to the human body. Its purpose is rooted in preserving this physical form because, without it, the mortal soul ceases to exist. Consequently, the mortal soul will not willingly harm its own body. Even individuals plagued by the most severe personality disorders rooted in the mortal soul—such as those associated with psychopathy or sociopathy—tend to direct their harm outward, at other people, rather than toward themselves. Self-preservation is paramount.

In contrast, the immortal spiritual soul does not share this instinctual bond with the human body. Originating from a realm devoid of physical forms or earthly definitions of life, the immortal soul views the body as no more than a temporary vessel. Its true purpose lies in cultivating spirituality, assimilating the spirit's divine qualities, and expressing those attributes in

the world. When this immortal spiritual soul dominates one's consciousness, the usual priorities of human existence—physical appearance, pleasure, diet, social
bonds—may lose their significance. To such an individual,
material comforts and bodily well-being can seem irrelevant
compared to the pursuit of spiritual growth.

An illustrative figure is Mahatma Gandhi. Gandhi was
known for his principled stance against materialism and the
pursuit of excess wealth. Influenced by Jain teachings such as
"aparigraha," which champions non-attachment and min-
imalism, Gandhi believed moral and spiritual advancement
held more value than accumulating possessions [4]. He ad-
vocated a simple life of limited material needs, seeing excess
consumption as a moral and spiritual hazard.

Individuals who embody this perspective treat the body as
a mere instrument to fulfill their spiritual mission on Earth.
They often exhibit characteristics indicative of the immortal
spiritual soul's influence, which can lead them to neglect their
physical selves. While such individuals harbor no malice and do
not wish to harm others, their intense inward spiritual focus can
sometimes manifest as detachment, antisocial behavior, or borderline personality traits. They may appear disconnected from
ordinary human pursuits, not because they are evil or violent,

---

4. (Parel, 2007) Gandhi's Philosophy and the Quest for Harmony. Cambridge University Press.

but because their energies center on transcendent goals rather than worldly interests.

In essence, when the immortal spiritual soul takes precedence, the human body's importance recedes into the background. This can foster admirable qualities like moral purity and spiritual intensity, yet it may also bring about unintended psychological and social challenges. It is a reminder that true balance lies in harmonizing the mortal soul's practical, life-sustaining instincts with the immortal soul's lofty, spirit-driven aspirations.

Positivity and Negativity

Many individuals find it far easier to gravitate toward negativity—harboring pessimism, selfishness, or indifference—because such dispositions yield immediate, though limited, rewards in this earthly existence. By contrast, embracing a loving, compassionate nature is more arduous and requires deliberate effort and self-discipline. Nevertheless, the fruits of such benevolent behavior extend beyond our material reality, bestowing spiritual benefits that persist into the spiritual realm.

As we cultivate the uplifting attributes of the immortal spiritual soul, these positive qualities begin to overshadow the inherently self-centered tendencies of the mortal animalistic soul. Over time, this moral and spiritual refinement produces a person who is empathetic and considerate of others. For most people, achieving a harmonious equilibrium—where both the mortal and immortal souls exert proportionate influence on the physical body and human consciousness—is a lifelong pursuit. This delicate balance ensures that we neither descend into animalistic self-interest nor sacrifice our psychological stability for uncompromised spirituality.

From a spiritual standpoint, a person deemed "evil" is one who completely lacks the influence of the immortal spiritual soul. In such an individual, the human consciousness remains firmly under the dominion of the mortal animalistic soul. With no room for the spiritual soul's positive traits to emerge, the capacity for kindness, empathy, or moral restraint diminishes, leading to a personality governed entirely by self-serving impulses. In extreme instances, these impulses may even corrupt the immortal soul itself. While ordinarily safeguarded by its divine essence, under severe conditions of unrestrained malevolence and hatred, the immortal soul can become tainted—losing spiritual purity and absorbing some of the mortal soul's negativity. This spiritual erosion is a grave event, as it can significantly diminish the immortal soul's inherent holiness and may permanently alter its essential nature.

Religious traditions across the world have long grappled with this concept of spiritual decay. Christianity, for example, frames it as a corruption arising from sin, traceable to the primordial transgression in the Garden of Eden. Within this framework, spiritual healing is attained through repentance, redemption, and embracing Christ's teachings, enabling the soul to cleanse

itself of its moral decay. In Islam, wrongdoings and malevolent actions metaphorically "blacken" or harden the heart—the
spiritual core of a person. Yet, through genuine repentance,
righteous deeds, and sincere prayer, the heart can be purified
once more. Judaism similarly provides a path from sin to virtue
through heartfelt repentance, prayer, fasting, acts of charity, and
renewed adherence to divine commandments. These religious
approaches converge on a central truth: regardless of initial spiritual contamination, there exists a means to rehabilitate, restore,
and elevate the soul.

> *By doing good, we plant
> seeds that keep growing
> beyond our physical exis-
> tence.*

In my estimation, only under extreme conditions—where
absolute evil and hatred reign—can the mortal soul's negative
aspects truly infect or deform the immortal soul. Since the immortal spiritual soul is imbued with divine spirit, it inherently
possesses a strong resistance against corruption. Moreover, it
is eternal and indestructible since the Higher Power does not
annihilate Their creations. The more influential the immortal
soul becomes within an individual, the more robust its defenses
against the mortal soul's self-serving nature.

In practice, most people achieve a relatively healthy balance of
both souls' influences. Education, moral guidance, and positive

environmental factors can curtail the mortal soul's narcissistic urges, ensuring that while we remain mindful of our physical needs, we do not allow these needs to overshadow ethical considerations or empathy. Simultaneously, nurturing the immortal soul's divine attributes—kindness, compassion, forgiveness, and justice—enables these virtues to overtake the baser instincts stemming from our mortal origin.

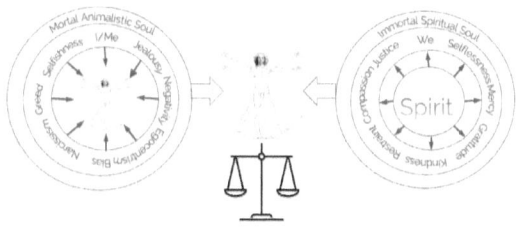

Figure 8: Soul Equilibrium

As we develop and strengthen these spiritual qualities, we don't just improve our own sense of well-being—we also treat others better, creating a more caring and morally grounded way of life. For most of us, this is a delicate balancing act. Neither the mortal nor the immortal soul ever truly goes away; both keep shaping our thoughts, decisions, and actions. The best we can aim for is to let the immortal spiritual soul quietly guide us. That way, even when life gets tough, we don't lose sight of the values that lead us toward kindness and doing what's right.

Of course, this balance isn't easy to maintain. Sometimes, it's hard to put our more noble qualities first because of outside stress, personal problems, or simply our own human flaws. Still, when we look back at the end of our lives, we can take comfort in the good we've done. Every act of understanding, compassion, and generosity has not only helped others—it has also strengthened our immortal spiritual soul. By doing good, we plant seeds that keep growing beyond our physical existence, carrying the best parts of our humanity and our connection to the divine into whatever lies ahead.

Chapter Eight

Soul Mates

Love is composed of a single soul inhabiting two bodies. - Aristotle

Do you believe in soul mates?

Some souls are meant to be together - they just are! I can't tell you why; it is not of this world. Maybe in the spirit world, these souls are bound together. Perhaps they have lived multiple lives together and been reincarnated repeatedly, only to search out each other. We don't know why some souls, or maybe all souls, search for their mates; however, I can tell you that soul mates do exist.

Some schools of thought[1] believe that the soul cannot find
its mate because it is cloaked in the human body and all the
baggage that comes with that. It is hidden behind layers of
humanity that have been influenced by a mortal soul that has no
interest in spirituality and connection to other souls. Accord-
ingly, to another soul, it will be unrecognizable. However, I do
not subscribe to this theory, and I say this because of personal
experience.

Most cultures and religions have some belief in soul mates.
For instance, in his dialogue "The Symposium,"[2] Plato describes a theory by the comic playwright Aristophanes. Humans
were initially created with four arms, four legs, and a head with
two faces. After an attempt to overpower the gods, Zeus split
them in half, condemning them to spend their lives searching
for the other half - their soulmate.

---

1. In Buddhism, the idea of a permanent, unchanging soul
   (or soul mate) does not align well with the fundamental
   principles of impermanence and non-self. Relationships
   are viewed more through the lens of interdependence and
   karmic connections. From a sociological perspective, the
   idea of a soul mate can be seen as a social construct that has
   evolved over time, influenced by cultural norms, literature,
   and media. The sociological view often emphasizes the
   importance of compatibility, communication, and shared
   effort in successful relationships over the notion of predes-
   tined matches.

2. (Bantas, 2010) Understanding Plato: The Symposium.

Also, in the Symposium, Plato explores various aspects of love. One of the speakers, Aristophanes, presents a myth explaining human desire for love as a quest for our "other half," from which we were separated in primordial times. Later, Socrates discusses the idea of love as a desire for the everlasting possession of the good and beautiful, extending it beyond physical attraction to the intellectual and spiritual realm.

What Aristophanes proposes is, in my opinion, not far from reality.

In traditional Hindu belief, the concept of a soulmate is often tied to the idea of arranged marriages and reincarnation. It's believed that souls are divinely matched to help them evolve spiritually through marital life. The 'Red String of Fate,' also referred to as the 'Red Thread of Marriage,' is an East Asian belief originating from Chinese legend. It is often thought of as an invisible red cord around the finger of those who are destined to meet one another in a certain situation as they are "their true love."

Few couples enjoy a soul that is bound together - almost mixed together would be a better analogy. As with soul mates, this is when you instinctively know when your partner is happy, sad, or angry, even if they are not near you. No words are required to connect in this way; it is a connection that is initiated at the level of the immortal soul, not a voluntary connection, a function of the soul that enables it to connect to another soul and never lose that connection even if the two people are on opposite sides of the world. When you connect with your immortal souls, you can communicate at a different level - the level of the soul itself.

Connections of the Spiritual Soul

Perhaps you've heard tales of soul mates discovering each other, or you've experienced this phenomenon yourself. If so, you're indeed fortunate. Throughout our lives, we might come across one or several soul mates. Recognizing such encounters, however, is entirely up to us. Are we brave enough to initiate a conversation with a stranger? Do we commit to the process of mutual discovery? While we might feel a natural pull towards each other – a gravitational force of sorts – the final push is ours to make. We must muster the courage to step beyond the inhibitions of our mortal soul and explore a profound connection.

Stumbling upon someone with whom you share a deep rapport doesn't necessarily promise a marriage or a romantic relationship. Often, we may realize that we are not personally ready or positioned to delve into any relationship. Yet, this connection simply implies that you've met someone with whom you resonate at a deeper level, a connection that intertwines one soul with another. Occasionally, you might find yourself crossing paths with a stranger on a bustling street, a fleeting glance exchanged, and suddenly, there's a profound connection, a bond that touches the very core of your soul. This connection, you realize, is reciprocal because the stranger, with barely a gesture, acknowledges it. It's an unspoken bond, a soulful encounter between two individuals who've chanced upon a soul mate. Although such incidents can be rare, they leave us with a comforting warmth, an assurance that we are not alone, that we've just brushed past someone we seem to know from another place, another time. Sometimes, such encounters with a soulmate can extend beyond a brief, fleeting moment into something more lasting.

When you have a high level of emotional intelligence and are empathetic towards other people, it seems more common that you would cross paths with a soul mate. In these cases, your soul is open and receptive to other people's souls. Recently, I met a new colleague. The moment this person walked into the room, our eyes hadn't even met, yet something in the air shifted; there was a sense that we knew each other, not in any physical way but on a spiritual level. We both knew it; we both acknowledged it, and we moved on with our meeting. Such encounters leave a residue that dissipates very slowly long after the encounter. We've all had moments like this, which makes me wonder: what does the soul understand about other souls that we, on a conscious level, do not?

A friend once described to me an encounter he had on his daily commuter train. The routine was always the same; he would board the train, more or less sit in the same seat, put on his headphones, and listen to music or read a book. The commute was about an hour, and he would often see the same people sitting in the same places.

One day, he boarded the train and found that his regular seat had already been taken; no problem. This happened quite often even though his station was only the second on the commuter line. On this day, he moved to a different carriage and sat down in the first empty seat that he could find. He recounts how he found himself sitting beside an orthodox Jewish woman. He in no way was orthodox and had no interest in any religion, yet he recognized her as belonging to a religiously observant group. Almost immediately, they started talking, he couldn't remember who initiated the conversation first, and it didn't really matter. When I spoke with him, he couldn't recall her name, exactly what she looked like, or any other physical attributes. None of that seemed to matter then, nor does it now.

He spoke to her non-stop for the full-hour commute - he had no idea about what, but the hour passed as if it were but a few minutes. He made a connection without even knowing anything about the other person. When he got off the train, he told me that they both recognized a sadness in their eyes that the train ride and, therefore, their connection was over. They left the train together and entered the station; both of them were going in different directions to different destinations. She gave him a long hug, kissed him very briefly on the lips, and was gone, swallowed in a mass of people heading away from him. He never saw her again, yet the simple connection they had made remained with him like a lingering residue long after it should have dissipated.

That connection was soul-to-soul; it ended as it should have, recognizing the connection and moving on. Neither of them was in any personal position to pursue anything more profound, and to do so would have been a mistake.

The profound spiritual connection

A soul-to-soul link is the most potent connection that can exist between two individuals.

Soul mates cross our paths occasionally; with some, we will be highly compatible, and there will be an undeniable profound connection. If our mutual circumstances support it, it is worth exploring a relationship. Otherwise, you acknowledge the connection somehow and move on, feeling better for having crossed paths with a soul you might have known in a past life, or from the spiritual realm. It's worth emphasizing that a soul mate can present as male, female, or identify as non-binary. As previously discussed, the spiritual realm does not operate on earthly constructs, so it doesn't recognize or concern itself with gender identity. While this touches upon a broader conversation about LGBTQI+ acceptance, that topic is beyond the scope of this chapter.

When you share a profound spiritual connection with someone, a bond that transcends the physical realm, you engage primarily with the individual's soul, not their outward persona. The physical appearance no longer dictates the intensity of your attraction towards them. This soul-to-soul link is the most potent connection that can exist between two individuals. You share their happiness and their sorrow; their anguish resonates within you during conflicts. This bond supersedes the physical, hinging on the interaction between souls at a spiritual level. When two souls connect, we may feel different emotions; however, the overwhelming emotion might be one of love – this is what the spiritual soul manifests.

The majority never experience this depth of connection. They might, at best, encounter someone they're physically drawn to, share intellectual compatibility, and develop affection. The soul-to-soul bond is relatively rare, but when it manifests, it fosters an extraordinary relationship where communication can happen with minimal words. This does not imply that couples with this profound connection are immune to disagreements; human nature and the mortal soul's inclination towards self-preservation ensure conflicts. The mortal soul can act as a dominant, self-centered force within the body, counterbalanced by the positive influences of the immortal spiritual soul.

Individuals sharing a soul-to-soul connection usually exhibit higher empathy and Emotional Intelligence (EQ)[3], as they're naturally receptive to a soul-level connection. If they hadn't been open to such a bond, they wouldn't have recognized it in the first place. Thus, their immortal spiritual soul has already exerted its influence over the mortal soul. At times, we might sense a strong connection with someone that isn't reciprocated, often because the other person's mortal soul dominates them, their EQ might be lower, or they may lack the necessary empathy to recognize another soul.

In a soul-to-soul connection, the physical aspects recede in importance. Traditional societal or self-imposed constraints regarding potential partners or spouses become irrelevant. The soul connection awakens a sentiment that renders all other relationship barriers obsolete. The most poignant love stories involve couples who defy social norms of class, religion, or race to unite. Such narratives aren't celebrated by accident; they embody the utopian world many of us aspire to witness. A soul-to-soul connection can disregard relationship taboos,

---

3. Emotional Intelligence (EQ or EI) refers to the ability to understand, use, and manage one's own emotions in positive ways to relieve stress, communicate effectively, empathize with others, overcome challenges and defuse conflict. It was popularized by psychologist and best-selling author Daniel Goleman in his 1995 book, "Emotional Intelligence" (Goleman, 2012).

transcend religious, social, cultural, and ethical divides, and unite two individuals in an unshakeable bond of love.

When I first met Elaine, I never imagined that a simple conversation on an airplane would change my life forever. It happened on a flight from Seattle to Burbank, a short two-hour journey. We were seated next to each other, and what began as polite small talk quickly turned into the most engaging conversation I had ever experienced. Time faded away; it felt as though we had known each other for years, not minutes. By the time we landed, I realized something astonishing: I had spent two hours deeply connecting with this woman, yet I hadn't looked at her face even once. Somehow, I already knew she was beautiful. I could sense her beauty in the rhythm of her voice and the warmth of her laughter.

When the plane touched down and we parted ways, it felt oddly difficult. It was as if I were leaving behind a part of myself. We agreed to meet again, just once, to see if what we'd felt was real or just a strange moment in time. We picked a place for lunch, nothing fancy—just a neutral spot to say a proper hello, see each other's faces, and then perhaps go our separate ways, both of us curious but wary.

The day I went to meet her, I realized I had no idea what she looked like. I scanned the restaurant nervously, worried we might miss each other. For a moment, I thought we might pass like ghosts in the same space, never realizing we were inches apart. But there she was—she recognized me immediately. I joined her at the table, my heart pounding, but the lunch itself was surprisingly calm and pleasant.

We were about to part, a moment that felt prematurely final, when I suddenly hugged her. This was unlike me; I wasn't a hugger, especially not with someone I'd only just met in person. But I reached out and pulled her close. It was awkward, unexpected, and yet perfect. I held her for a second that seemed to stretch into eternity. And in that embrace, something happened—something neither of us could have prepared for.

We both felt it. A sensation that something was being pulled from within us, and yet not quite removed—more like rearranged. It was as if a piece of each of us left our own bodies and settled into the other. There was no pain, just a strange, electric awareness. When we let go, we looked at each other, startled, silently acknowledging that something immense had just occurred. I walked away slowly, my mind spinning. All I could think was: "Something has changed. No," said a voice in my head, "not something; everything has changed."

> *The connection of our immortal spiritual souls is what brought us together - we found spiritual compatibility.*

I had never been the type to need another person constantly. I enjoyed my solitude, valued my personal space, and felt comfortable on my own terms. But after that moment, being away from Elaine felt wrong—almost unhealthy. Even now, if we're apart for too long, it's like my soul grows weary. When I'm near her, I'm at peace. I sense her emotions without her speaking a word. If she's sad, I feel it. If she's worried or confused, I know it instantly, and she knows when I'm off balance as well. It's as if our souls are two components that need each other to maintain a perfect equilibrium.

What we found that day wasn't just a soul mate in the usual sense; it was "The soul mate," the one destined to be with us through all lifetimes and in the spiritual realm beyond this existence. On that day, our immortal souls merged—two bodies, one soul. Ever since, we've been able to feel each other no matter the distance. Whether I'm close by or half a world away, I can tap into her feelings, and she can sense mine. There's no need for words to know what the other is thinking; we simply know. It's as if we share the same wavelength, a secret language written between our hearts.

We can't deny what we witnessed. We saw it happen, we felt it happen, and we are still living it every day. It remains the most profound and mysterious experience of my life—the moment I realized I'd found my other half, not just in this world, but in all the worlds to come.

Social Segregation – The Soul Mate Killer

The sad thing is that in this life, we are bound by many ir-relevant and outdated social norms regarding who we should meet, who we should date, who is in our social circle, and who we should eventually marry. We restrict ourselves to a small subset of humanity, be it ethnicity, race, religion, color, social standing, nationality, or any other of a thousand different cat-egorizations. Your soul mate may not be in this limited social group; by limiting your interactions to people who are "like" you, you are, in effect, catering to the needs of the mortal soul. The mortal soul is interested in your survival. It makes sense to keep company with people who look and think like yourself, to bond on a superficial level. Connecting with a group of people who look and think alike increases the chances that the human body will survive longer and have its needs met. It eliminates the factor of the unknown. Being a member of such a group also provides much-needed validation to a mortal soul that is naturally insecure due to its mortality.

The immortal spiritual soul has absolutely no regard for gender, social group, religion, or ethnicity - this is a construct that the mortal soul requires to guarantee the human body's survival. We know that people group together instinctively to survive; this is ingrained in our DNA from the earliest times when you could only survive as part of the collective. However, your soulmate may be of a different nationality, religion, or ethnicity - social groupings are a construct of the mortal world and, therefore, are irrelevant to the immortal soul. To recognize the connection and allow your souls to mingle, what is relevant is an openness, a belief in something bigger than yourself, an immortal soul that has been allowed to grow to dominate the selfishness and restrictions of the mortal soul.

The spiritual soul has no regard for gender, social group, religion, or ethnicity.

Elaine and I are direct opposites in every way possible. I am white, and she is Asian. I am Jewish, she is Christian, I am English, and she is Korean; we have different theologies, different backgrounds, and eat different foods, yet we believe in the same basic principles that govern our lives, the key one being that there is more to this life than just ourselves. We could meet and recognize each other regardless of our differences because our spiritual souls were exposed and could connect; we are both empathetic and spiritual. Our differences became irrelevant. We didn't have to look at each other to build a connection; the physical is the domain of the mortal soul - a connection of our immortal souls; our spiritual souls are what brought us together - our spiritual compatibility.

Bonds of the Mortal Soul

It's widely understood that soul mates can form a connection at the spiritual level between immortal souls. However, can a mortal soul establish a bond with another mortal soul? The response is affirmative, and it's a much more frequent occurrence than the soul mate bond at the spiritual level - it's a simpler connection to establish.

As discussed earlier, the mortal soul revolves around the self: "I want this; I like this; I need this." It's a self-centric soul preoccupied with fulfilling the needs of the human body. These needs may range from survival through nutrition to companionship and procreation. A significant portion of what we often perceive as love can be described as "selfish love." This type of love is characterized by a situation where our chosen partner fulfills our needs. They satisfy a need we possess, for example, "He gives me a sense of validation," or "I am fond of her because she caters to my needs." However, genuine love, love that comes from the immortal spiritual soul, shifts the focus from our needs to the needs of the other person. It essentially involves prioritizing the other person's needs over our own, such as "I have the ability to make her happy" or "I can provide for her." Viewing our partner from this perspective allows us to cultivate a deeper relationship where the emphasis is on attending to each other's needs instead of solely our own.

The attractions governed by the mortal soul are typically superficial, rooted in physical attributes: Is she attractive? Does he dress well? Does she meet my standards of physical allure? While thoughtfulness might be appreciated, it might not be the primary concern initially. Relationships built on physical appeal, common interests, and an understanding of each other's physical needs but devoid of any spiritual bond could lack a deeper purpose that provides for a long-term relationship. Such a partnership might offer companionship for weeks, months, or even years. However, in the end, they'll discover the absence of depth and will no longer be able to cater to the superficial demands of the mortal soul. This is a common relationship archetype, explaining why numerous couples resort to infidelity or divorce to satisfy the physical urges of the mortal soul with another partner. If such a relationship perseveres, it's often due to the shared objective of procreation, where the shared duty of raising children binds the couple. Once the children depart, the couple often realizes their commonalities are as sparse as they were pre-children, occasionally leading to separation.

> *Genuine love, a love that emanates from the spiritual soul, shifts the focus from our needs to the needs of the other person.*

Most relationships don't fall entirely into one extreme or the other. It's important to recognize that the immortal spiritual soul often tempers the impulses of the mortal soul, creating a balanced dynamic. When the immortal soul positively influences the human consciousness, it brings spirituality into the relationship, strengthening the bond between two people. While physical attraction or shared experiences might initiate a relationship, it's the influence of the immortal soul and the spiritual connection it fosters that truly sustains it.

As couples move beyond the initial thrill of physical attraction and the excitement of early dating, life's responsibilities inevitably take center stage. Relationships that rely solely on the needs of the mortal soul—physical attraction, validation, or shared activities—are bound to weaken over time. In contrast, relationships enriched by the immortal spiritual soul's deeper bond, often referred to as a soul mate connection, can endure and grow stronger indefinitely.

However, the opposite is also true. Even in relationships with strong spiritual bonds, the mortal soul can exert its influence. Physical desires, while natural, remain the most potent force of the mortal soul. These urges can test even the most spiritually grounded individuals. Although spiritual people may resist acting on such impulses, the mortal soul's influence persists, as this is its fundamental purpose.

For a relationship to thrive long-term, it's essential to nurture love and mutual respect. Open communication, focused attention, and active efforts to grow and maintain your connection with your partner help protect against the mortal soul's negative influences. By doing so, you close the door to selfish or destructive tendencies.

Not everyone finds a soul mate, but that doesn't mean they can't experience a fulfilling and happy relationship. Love, respect, and friendship form the foundation of many lasting partnerships. Who knows? Perhaps such relationships are where soul mates are created in the first place.

Chapter Nine

Interfaith Challages

We've envisioned an inclusive society, one that aligns with the Divine's vision—a world where barriers crumble, where outdated societal and religious norms no longer dictate whom we meet, date, befriend, or marry. It's a beautiful ideal, a world without segregation based on faith, culture, or tradition. However, I must acknowledge that breaking down those walls and stepping beyond our comfort zones is far easier to write about than to put into practice. Change requires courage, understanding, and a willingness to confront deeply rooted beliefs.

The story that follows is the story of Elaine, my wife, and myself, told from both of our perspectives. Ours is just one narrative among thousands, each filled with its own joys and struggles. There are countless tales of families torn apart by the decision to marry outside their faith or even outside a specific denomination within that faith. Stories of parents mourning what they saw as a loss when their children chose a different path. Stories of silence replacing connection, of grandparents never meeting their grandchildren, and of relationships severed due to rigid adherence to tradition.

Our story, however, is one of bridging divides, of embracing love and mutual respect despite the differences that could have kept us apart. It is a story that highlights the challenges and triumphs of stepping beyond inherited norms, and it serves as a reminder that the work of building an inclusive society begins with each of us, one relationship at a time.

Elaine's Story

Navigating an interfaith relationship comes with its unique set of challenges, yet it is precisely these challenges that have paved the way for unexpected and profound rewards. We stand by each other in our distinct religious practices, discovering joy and unity in our collective journey toward understanding and honoring the Divine.

God is the cornerstone in our lives, seamlessly interwoven into every aspect — from the quiet gratitude expressed at our dinner table to the exaltation of nature's wonders during our outdoor escapades. This shared reverence elevates our experiences, transforming routine moments into opportunities for spiritual connection and growth.

Our union has not been universally embraced; we've encountered everything from skepticism to outright hostility. Accusations of forsaking my Christian faith for marrying a man of Jewish heritage have been hurled my way, just as he has endured slurs for his choice to build a life with someone outside Judaism. I've been told I'm not a true Christian and have gone crazy for marrying a Jew.

Among the dissenters was a friend from my seminary days; for the sake of this narrative, we'll call her Susan. Our companionship spanned more than twenty years. We shared memories and experiences and forged a bond I believed was unbreakable. She was initially intrigued by my choice of a life partner, diving into research about his Jewish heritage with a zest that signaled support. Yet, as her understanding deepened, so did a chasm between us.

Without warning, Susan's warmth gave way to an icy distance, her curiosity replaced by a barrier of disapproval. The foundational disagreement over the legitimacy of interfaith relationships proved insurmountable. Her inability to reconcile my love for someone outside the Christian fold with her theology led her to a stark conclusion: that my choices rendered me unworthy of the friendship we had nurtured for decades. And just like that, the rich tapestry of our shared history unraveled.

For me, Judaism was a blank slate; I had no preconceived perceptions as to the nature of the religion and the Jewish people. I was an open book, ready to absorb everything about God's firstborn. Gideon was equally excited to introduce me to the richness of his religion, the beauty of the traditions, and the ancient prayers and rituals anchored in the ancient scriptures of the Old Testament.

When I first accompanied Gideon to the conservative synagogue he attended in North San Fernando Valley, near Los Angeles, I was introduced to a new world of tradition and community. Gideon, substituting for the Rabbi one weekend, provided a sermon that demonstrated his deep knowledge and eloquent speaking skills, leaving me deeply impressed. Witnessing the ancient practice of reading from the Torah scroll, a tradition tracing back over three millennia, was an eye-opening experience for me.

The synagogue, which functioned as much more than just a place of worship, was a hub for a dynamic youth community, proud of their heritage and religion. Gideon's decade-long involvement in the synagogue, including his role on the board of governors, gave me insight into this vibrant community. His extensive volunteering and participation in communal events allowed me to forge connections with many of its members.

However, I gradually recognized certain limitations inherent in Conservative Judaism, especially concerning the participation of non-Jews in specific religious rituals. These included restrictions on handling the Torah scroll and participation in specific ceremonial roles. While these practices were understandable and logical to the Jewish congregation, they contrasted sharply with the inclusive ethos of my own church.

There were accommodations for non-Jewish attendees, like allowing them to open the ark housing the Torah scrolls. Yet, they were prohibited from touching the scrolls themselves. I also learned about the limitations imposed on non-Jews regarding their involvement in synagogue management. It turns out that depending upon the specific Jewish denomination, acceptance of non-Jews and the roles they are allowed to play in the synagogue vary greatly. Conservative Judaism was attempting to strike a balance between the practice of their traditional Jewish values and the fact that many of their followers are interfaith families. The synagogue Gideon attended had a Rabbi who fell more on the orthodox end of the religious spectrum and, as a result, promoted a less inclusive theology.

As our marriage progressed, it became increasingly evident that I, and by extension, Gideon, faced subtle forms of discrimination within this community. This ranged from a greeter deliberately ignoring my presence to hearing derogatory terms like 'Shiksa' and 'Goy,' which were used pejoratively to emphasize my outsider status, especially given my role as a pastor.

Gideon's disappointment with the discrimination we faced at the synagogue was palpable. Despite his efforts to address these issues with the synagogue leadership, the persistent discrimination ultimately led us to make the difficult decision to leave. Gideon made it clear to me that the actions of a few individuals did not represent the Jewish people as a whole, and he was determined to ensure that I had a positive and welcoming experience within his faith community.

We searched for a Jewish place of worship that would provide us with inclusivity and, above all else, a spiritual connection to God. Orthodox Judaism was a non-starter since I would be even more discriminated against as a woman and specifically as a non-Jew. Reform Judaism provided acceptance; however, there was no spirituality there and no depth of learning. Eventually, we found a unique community that promoted acceptance and spirituality in their services.

Our journey in search of a spiritual community led us to a synagogue in Santa Monica that promised an inclusive and open approach to worship. The services there were welcoming to all, with the Rabbi, an insightful and knowledgeable woman, delivering well-researched sermons that resonated with contemporary issues. Accompanied by a spiritually connected, talented live band, the overall experience was enriching and seemed aligned with our interfaith values. We were particularly moved by the High Holiday services held outdoors, which Gideon described as the most spiritual he had ever experienced. It felt like we had finally found a place where we belonged.

However, as Hanukkah and Christmas approached, a disheartening incident occurred. During a service, the Rabbi mentioned her invitation to participate in a city-sponsored Hanukkah candle-lighting event that happened to fall on Christmas Eve. But, to our surprise and growing discomfort, she repeatedly avoided saying the word "Christmas," referring to it indirectly and awkwardly as "THAT...THAT..." Initially, I thought it might be a humorous approach, but it became painfully clear that she was deliberately avoiding the term. The situation escalated to the point where a member of the band had to exclaim "Christmas!" for her, to which she only replied, "Yeah...THAT!"

This episode left us both shocked and deeply disappointed. As I shared with Gideon, it was difficult for me to align myself with a community led by someone who seemed to find the mere mention of "Christmas" distasteful or taboo, as if it were a curse word. This attitude starkly contradicted the claim of accepting interfaith families. It was a sharp reminder that despite outward appearances of openness, underlying biases and lack of genuine respect for other faiths could still be prevalent. Like our experience at the first synagogue, this apparent openness did not extend to genuinely embracing interfaith relationships, leaving us again feeling disconnected and unacknowledged in our quest for a spiritual home where both our faiths were respected.

No matter how diligently we searched, our quest to find a Jewish place of worship that embodied both inclusivity and spirituality proved to be a challenging endeavor. Such a congregation, one that would fully embrace and nurture our interfaith journey, remained elusive.

My initial neutral perspective on the Jewish community had been indelibly affected. Gideon stressed that my negative experiences were with a limited group of individuals, not representative of the whole. Yet, despite his reassurances, I couldn't shake the feeling of irony that a people who had endured millennia of discrimination were, in these instances, displaying discriminatory behaviors themselves.

Gideon's Story

Not long after I married Elaine we were looking forward to traveling to Israel together to celebrate my daughter's wedding. It was a few days prior to the departure that I had a phone call from a family member. The person demanded that I not take Elaine to the wedding out reverence for the Rabbi who would be conditioning the service. "It's not appropriate that the Rabbi will be in the precensnce of a shiksa who is also a pastor," this person told me.

This conversation was etched in my memory, marking a profound realization. My wife, whom I loved deeply and considered my soul mate, the woman who brought joy and completeness to my life, would always be viewed with skepticism and prejudice by some within my faith community. Regardless of surface-level acceptance or expressions of joy about our union, underlying bias and derogatory remarks lingered, spoken by family, friends, or strangers alike.

Despite encountering opposition from some, it was heartening to know that many in my immediate family wholeheartedly embraced our marriage. Their support was a beacon of hope, especially considering the long and arduous journey I had endured to find true happiness. After two failed marriages, countless heartaches, and a lifelong soul-searching journey, I had finally found Elaine, a partner for the latter part of my life.

This confrontation with the family member prompted a significant shift in my perspective. Why should anyone dictate who is suitable for me based on ethnicity or religion? Such narrow viewpoints had no place in determining my happiness.

It was a definitive turning point. I resolved then and there to disregard others' opinions about our marriage. My path forward with Elaine was clear – we would carve our future based on our beliefs, shared spiritual path, and love for each other. From that moment, our journey would no longer be swayed by external perceptions of what was deemed appropriate. We were committed to building a life together, guided by our own convictions and mutual respect.

This incident had the side-effect of crystalizing in my mind the path forward, a path that would define how we lived our joint lives together. No longer would we focus on the exclusivity of our religions; from now on, we would focus on our spirituality and shared connection with God. We would live our lives for God and not for the acceptance of others, be they our family or our friends.

Our lives were filled with individuals who embraced us unconditionally, genuinely accepting who we were. There was a natural curiosity about the dynamics of our relationship, but rejection was rare; the majority welcomed our union with open arms. Just as certain members of my family and some in my Jewish community had turned away from us, Elaine, too, faced the sting of rejection from some of her longstanding friends. I knew this rejection deeply wounded her.

Elaine's family stood as a shining example of acceptance. Her parents, initially taken aback and saddened by her decision to divorce her first husband, whom they saw as a respectful and kind person, were unaware of the underlying struggles Elaine had faced in that relationship. When she explained the reasons behind the divorce, they came to terms with it, albeit with a hesitancy about her remarrying.

Their surprise was evident when Elaine later revealed she was in a new relationship. As for me, the thought of meeting her family, especially given their Korean-American background, was a source of nervous anticipation. I diligently prepared, asking Elaine for advice on cultural etiquette and even learning some basic Korean phrases to demonstrate my sincere intentions.

Our first meeting with her parents took place in Seattle during the COVID-19 pandemic. Elaine's mother greeted us, masked and initially hiding her hands, at the entrance of their home. Before we could step inside and take off our shoes, she humorously yet unexpectedly sprayed us with disinfectant. This quirky and amusing gesture immediately dissolved any initial awkwardness and served as a memorable introduction to her family.

Despite their deep Christian faith and active involvement in their church, Elaine's family embraced me wholeheartedly. They extended warmth, care, and, most importantly, respect for my distinct religious beliefs. Their acceptance deeply moved me, given our differing backgrounds in race, nationality, and religion.

In a similar vein, most of Elaine's closest friends, including some who were clergy, welcomed our relationship. They not only accepted our union but also offered their blessings, adding to the circle of support and acceptance in our lives. The predominant sentiment among those close to Elaine was one of genuine happiness for her newfound contentment and joy in our relationship. They were delighted to see her in love and experiencing happiness. Many expressed their gratitude directly to me, thanking me for being a source of such positivity in Elaine's life. This widespread acceptance and appreciation deeply affirmed the love and connection we shared.

Growing up, my understanding was clear-cut: church was a place for Christians, while synagogues were for Jews. This distinction was a fundamental part of my Jewish upbringing.

Consequently, when I first began attending church, it wasn't for religious reasons but rather to stand by my wife in her ministry. By occupying the front pew during services, I was not just offering her my unwavering support; I was also helping to elevate her status in the eyes of her congregation. Our presence there represented a unified front: she was the Pastor and spiritual leader, and I was her supportive partner. This dynamic felt right, and it remains the primary reason I continue to be a regular fixture in the front pew, directly supporting her in her spiritual leadership.

Discovering how Elaine crafted her weekly church services truly surprised me. My background in Judaism had accustomed me to a very different approach to religious services. In Judaism, services follow a centuries-old, unchanging structure, with prayers recited from a Siddur—a prayer book filled with texts that Jews have used for thousands of years worldwide.

So, learning that Elaine composed her prayers, decided on the service's theme, and selected the music was eye-opening for me. However, I quickly came to appreciate how she could create a service that embarked on a profound spiritual journey. I genuinely admire and cherish her talent for crafting prayers, sometimes even spontaneously, that resonate deeply with the soul.

My ongoing struggle with references to Jesus in Christian worship is rooted in a deeply ingrained aspect of my consciousness. As a proud Jew, I value my heritage immensely and don't shy away from expressing my religious and cultural identity.

The central distinction between Christianity and Judaism, for me, lies in the belief in Jesus as the son of God, a concept that I do not embrace as part of my Jewish faith (there are other differences, but this is the key principle that I struggle to accept).

Despite this fundamental difference, I hold a deep respect for the significant role and influence that Jesus has in Christianity. My respect acknowledges the profound impact and the spiritual power that belief in Jesus holds for Christians, including my wife and her congregation. This respectful acknowledgment allows me to support my wife in her ministry and engage with her community while maintaining my own religious beliefs and identity.

For Elaine and me, navigating the vast differences between our religions has been surprisingly fluid and natural. We approach our deep-seated theological differences with an attitude of mutual respect, a desire to learn, and a willingness to understand. Through countless hours of discussion, we have enlightened each other and opened our minds to perspectives that once seemed unfathomable.

These conversations have allowed us to bridge even the most daunting divides in our religious beliefs. Our experience is a testament to the power of communication and empathy in overcoming differences, highlighting that with the right approach, even the most significant theological differences can be peacefully reconciled in a respectful and loving relationship.

Chapter Ten

Acts of God

You can't connect the dots looking forward; you can only connect them looking backwards. So, you have to trust that the dots will somehow connect in your future. You have to trust in something - your gut, destiny, life, karma, whatever. This approach has never let me down, and it has made all the difference in my life. - Steve Jobs

Recently, a young man known to my wife passed away unexpectedly. He was a vibrant 45-year-old, generally in good health, but in a sudden and shocking turn of events, he was gone. These tragic occurrences aren't infrequent, and we're left reeling, trying to comprehend how someone so youthful and robust could depart so abruptly. Medical explanations often cite strokes or heart attacks, as in this young man's case. He was a kindhearted individual, always ready to assist others and devoutly involved in the church, the epitome of Christian virtue.

Why, then, do such good souls depart so prematurely?

Kabbalah[1] offers an intriguing perspective, attributing the unexpected deaths of infants and young people to soul reincarnation and the concept of "*Tikkun Olam*"[2] - a commitment to improving the world. Every soul is tasked with reaching a high spiritual level, achieved through deeds promoting *Tikkun Olam*. Once a soul accomplishes this, there is no need for soul reincarnation or further physical existence. Although this Kabbalistic view helps frame sudden death in a positive light, it is understandably little consolation for those grieving the loss.

While I concur with the Kabbalah's principles about death and soul reincarnation, I believe it doesn't sufficiently address the sudden death of young people. It doesn't distinctly explain the divergence between the deaths of younger and older individuals.

> *Why do bad things happen to good people?*

---

1. Kabbalah is a form of Jewish mysticism that interprets the Bible in an esoteric manner. Kabbalah seeks to define the nature of the universe and the human being, the nature and purpose of existence, and various other ontological questions.

2. Tikkun Olam is a concept in Judaism that translates literally to "repairing the world." It has come to denote social action and the pursuit of social justice, inspired by the idea that it's humanity's responsibility to partner with God to improve the world and make it a better place.

As we learned from our exploration of the two-soul theory, the mortal soul is primarily concerned with the physical body's well-being, whereas the immortal soul is indifferent to bodily concerns. Therefore, it is highly unlikely for the mortal soul, aiming for self-preservation, to prompt sudden death. This leaves two possibilities - the immortal soul or The divine spirit within us.

However, considering how difficult it is for the immortal soul to overrule the physical body and how such overruling often results in mental health issues rather than physical cessation, we are inclined to believe The divine spirit plays a critical role in these sudden departures.

The spirit is the divine spark—the breath of life—that animates our physical bodies. Without this sacred essence, life ceases to exist. Yet, this divine spirit is not something we control; it is governed by a Higher Power, operating on a level far beyond human understanding.

The mortal soul, rooted in the physical world, is constrained by time and space. It thrives within the tangible, measurable realities of life. By contrast, the immortal soul and the spirit exist outside these boundaries, dwelling in a realm that is timeless and spaceless. This fundamental difference makes it almost impossible for us to fully grasp the nature of their existence or the plans of the Higher Power that governs them.

Our understanding is inherently limited, confined to what we can observe and process through human perception. The actions and intentions of a Higher Power often remain mysterious to us. While we may glimpse patterns and purpose in hindsight, the broader scope of divine will—the grand design that unfolds across eternity—remains largely hidden. It's a humbling reminder that our lives are part of something far greater, a plan that transcends the confines of our mortal comprehension.

In Exodus 33:20, during a dialogue between God and Moses, God states: "But," He said, "You cannot see My face, for no one may see Me and live." According to some interpretations, it signifies our human limitation of not being able to foresee the future or understand the divine plan in its entirety. We can only grasp past events, not the full scope of time and space, as perceived by a divine entity.

The untimely demise of a young person, while deeply traumatic for those left behind, can bring about significant change. It propels people onto different paths, potentially altering history and steering humanity toward the divine plan's fulfillment. Although painful, we must remember that the body's death is not the end of the immortal soul. The immortal soul, having played its part in the divine plan, has likely attained a high spiritual state and will live on. This is, in essence, a great honor and the ultimate achievement for the immortal soul.

Divine Plan vs Free Will

If The Divine has predetermined humanity's path, what, then, is the purpose of free will? We have understood that humanity's free will influences the immortal soul: the actions we take in our lives affect the spirituality of the immortal soul. However, many also believe that there is an overreaching divine plan for humanity—a tension arises between these two fundamental theologies. How can we reconcile two seemingly disparate approaches to the Divine? This section just scratches the surface of what might be one of theology's greatest paradoxes. However, it is key to spiritual growth.

Amongst the religions that stand out in their stance on there being a predefined plan is the Protestant branch of Calvinism. Following the teachings of John Calvin (1509-1564), they hold a belief in predestination, which asserts that God has already chosen who will be saved and who will be damned, regardless of their actions on Earth.

Calvinism has had a significant impact on the development of Protestant theology and has been influential in the formation of several Christian denominations, such as the Presbyterian Church and the Reformed Church.

In his book, [3] "Institutes of the Christian Religion," (Calvin, 2017) Calvin defines the theology of "Unconditional Election":

> *"By predestination, we mean the eternal decree of God, by which he determined with himself whatever he wished to happen with regard to every man. All are not created on equal terms, but some are preordained to eternal life, others to eternal damnation; and, accordingly, as each has been created for one or the other of these ends, we say that he has been predestinated to life or to death."*
>
> Unconditional Election: Book III, Chapter 21, Section 1

In this passage, Calvin asserts that predestination is an eternal decree of God, in which he has determined the eternal fate of every individual. Again, this concept is central to the doctrine of Unconditional Election, which holds that God's choice of who will be saved is based solely on his divine will, not on any merit or condition of the individual.

It is important to mention that most Protestant denominations do not adhere to this theology and generally believe that a person's ultimate destination is defined by their acts in

---

3. Calvin, J., Beveridge, H., & Hendrickson Publishers. (2017). Institutes of the Christian religion. Hendrickson Publishers.

this world as well as their acceptance of Jesus as their savior. In fact, a person's free will and what they do with that gift is central to most Christian theologies. An additional Christian viewpoint posits that when free will choices are made that align with God's will and purpose, that person will be endowed with the goodness of eternal life.

When compared to Calvinism, Judaism presents a distinctly contrasting view on the concept of free will and divine intervention. A foundational principle in Judaism is the belief that every individual has the ability to choose between good and evil. This concept is not just a philosophical stance; it is the cornerstone of Jewish law and ethics. Without free will, the accountability that underpins moral and legal responsibility in Judaism would collapse. Deuteronomy 30:19 encapsulates this idea: *"I have set before you life and death, blessing and curse; therefore, choose life."*

Judaism holds a nuanced view that embraces both free will and divine providence, creating a delicate balance between human autonomy and God's omniscience. God is seen as deeply involved in the affairs of the world, with knowledge of all events—past, present, and future. This raises a profound theological question: if God already knows the future, how can humans genuinely exercise free will? This tension has been a central theme in Jewish philosophical and theological thought.

Many Jewish scholars suggest that divine involvement operates on multiple levels. Some events are directly willed by God as part of the divine plan, while others unfold according to natural law or human choice. This allows for a degree of human autonomy while maintaining the overarching framework of divine providence. This means that while The Divine progresses a plan by guiding humanity in a general direction, They do not involve themselves in humanity's day-to-day decisions – this provides for humanity's free will to be asserted.

Maimonides (Rambam), one of Judaism's most influential medieval philosophers, tackled this paradox in his writings. He argued that God's knowledge is fundamentally different from human knowledge. While humans perceive events sequentially, God exists outside of time and perceives all of existence simultaneously. This unique perspective allows God to know all possible outcomes without infringing on human free will. For Maimonides, this distinction preserves the compatibility of divine foreknowledge and human agency, affirming both God's omniscience and humanity's moral responsibility.

In the "Guide for the Perplexed,"[4] (Maimonides, 2000) particularly in Part III, Chapter 20, Maimonides touches upon the topic of God's knowledge. He writes:

> *"God does not know with a knowledge that is external to Him, in the same way as we possess a knowledge that is external to us. He and His knowledge are one."*
>
> Maimonides M. Guide for the Perplexed

---

4. Maimonides, Moses. 2000. The Guide for the Perplexed.

Maimonides' resolution of the tension between God's omniscience and human free will centers on the idea that God's knowledge is utterly distinct from human knowledge. For Maimonides, God's knowledge is not a separate attribute but inseparable from His essence—an integral part of God's being. This is a critical theological point, as Maimonides, committed to strict monotheism, seeks to avoid any suggestion of multiplicity or change in God's nature.

By highlighting the fundamental difference between divine and human knowledge, Maimonides bypasses the seeming contradiction. Were God's knowledge similar to ours, it would suggest that God's awareness of future choices would predetermine those choices, thus nullifying free will. Instead, Maimonides argues that God's knowledge transcends human comprehension, existing in a realm beyond the constraints of time and space. This allows God to know every choice a person will make without interfering with the freedom of those choices.

The mechanics of how divine foreknowledge and human free will coexist remain a mystery even within Maimonides' framework. He acknowledges the limitations of human understanding, emphasizing that finite minds cannot fully grasp the infinite nature of divine knowledge. Nevertheless, he firmly maintains that these two principles are not only compatible but essential to uphold. Human free will ensures moral responsibility, while God's omniscience underscores divine perfection and unity.

Through this perspective, Maimonides preserves the integrity of Jewish theology, allowing for a God who is all-knowing yet does not infringe on the autonomy of human beings. This delicate balance reinforces the idea that humans are moral agents, accountable for their actions, even as they exist within the scope of a divine plan.

Souls are not preordained by God for salvation or exclusion; rather, all souls are equal in their divine origin.

Judaism affirms both the omnipotence and omniscience of God while also upholding the essential principle of free will. This balance between divine foreknowledge and human agency has been a focal point of Jewish philosophical and theological exploration. The understanding of these concepts often depends on individual beliefs, personal experiences, and the specific Jewish teachings one follows.

From the perspective of the soul and spirit, free will is evident. The mortal soul tends to pull us toward self-serving instincts, while the immortal soul urges us toward higher, selfless actions. Yet, the ultimate decision rests with human free will—our ability to choose whether to follow the path of selfishness or altruism. This gift of free will, granted by God, allows humans to act independently, free from direct divine intervention in daily choices, yet still part of a grander divine plan. This plan, while incomprehensible in its entirety, subtly encourages humanity toward actions that align with its fulfillment.

I believe the theological framework of Calvinism, with its emphasis on predestination, doesn't align with the inherent nature of human free will. Free will enables us to be partners in God's ongoing creation, reflecting divine qualities through our choices. The decisions we make in our earthly lives directly shape the state of our immortal souls. These souls are not pre-ordained by God for salvation or exclusion; rather, all souls are equal in their divine origin. Their spiritual growth depends on the experiences and choices they encounter during their time within the human body. This view underscores the collaborative, dynamic relationship between humanity and the divine, where each soul contributes uniquely to the unfolding of the divine plan.

Chapter Eleven

Devine Synchronicity

Throughout much of my life, I seldom reflected on where I might fit within God's grand design. The mere notion that I could be a tiny cog in Their vast cosmic mechanism seemed far-fetched. What could I possibly offer that would matter to such a supreme entity? Any other line of thought felt hubristic to me.

In alignment with many prevalent religious doctrines, I always maintained the belief that we possessed free will and that our choices shaped our destiny and what awaited us in the afterlife. Beyond this framework, I didn't delve much into the matter. But then, Elaine entered my life.

I've touched upon the moment Elaine and I crossed paths and the inexplicable mingling of our souls in chapter eight. Yet, there's a depth to our story that wasn't fully explored in that account.

Indeed, numerous circumstances paved the way for our serendipitous encounter on that airplane. A sequence of events, both in my life and hers, had been unfolding, possibly for years leading up to that moment. Like a meticulously arranged set of dominoes, every event cascaded perfectly into the next. Had even a single occurrence deviated from its course, our paths would never have intersected in that precise manner.

The realization that we can now trace back and discern the patterns that led to our union astonishes us. It bears the hallmark of a divine hand guiding our destinies. But what I aim to elaborate on here transcends this recognition. When viewed within the broader framework of a divine blueprint, not just for us but for all of humanity, the implications are staggering. It challenges many established tenets of religious philosophy.

Elaine was frozen in her car, heart racing, every emotion crashing over her like tumultuous waves. She'd just bid me farewell, and every fiber of her being was resonating with the intensity of what she had just realized. She had arrived with the intent to sever the bond that had just begun to form, a task that should've been simple. She had worked it all out in her mind prior to the meeting, and up until that last moment, everything had gone according to the plan. Then came that last unexpected revelation, which now left her reeling.

"Why did he draw my attention to his leg?" she pondered, her breath uneven. The weight of recognition pressed heavily on her as she connected the dots, sending shivers racing across her skin. "How could this be real?" The Divine's synchronicity was overwhelming. "What was God telling me and why?" she questioned.

When I was three years old, I broke my leg. Amazingly, I remember in clear detail every moment of that excruciating ordeal. I remember how my brother and I were playing in our bedroom. I remember how my mother had told us not to go upstairs since she had just finished cleaning the bedrooms. Our youthful energy was boundless; we darted around the room, colliding in joyous laughter, our voices intertwining in sheer delight. My brother stands out in my mind, clear as day. Being two years older, he seemed like a fountain of wisdom to my young eyes. To me, he was the epitome of all I aspired to be. In his presence, I felt there was so much he could teach me. My admiration for him didn't wane for many years after that; if anything, it deepened. He was not just my elder brother; he was my role model, and back in those youthful days, I cherished him profoundly.

On that fateful day, our bedroom became our playground. Despite our mother's explicit instruction not to venture upstairs, we were irresistibly drawn to a place where we could run and have fun without our mother's admonishment. 'Horseplay,' she used to call it; every time we would run around in the house chasing each other playfully, she would admonish us, "Stop that horseplay right now," she would shout. As we dashed and playfully collided, a particularly hard bump sent me crashing to the floor. The immediate surge of pain in my leg was overwhelming. Through my tears, I saw my brother's face clouded with concern, asking if I was okay. But moments later, he was gone. He didn't summon help or call out to our mother; he just vanished. A feeling of helplessness overcame me; in my acute pain, all I could think about was, "Where's my brother? Where has he gone? Did he go to call mummy?"

Desperate and in pain, I used my arms to drag myself to the landing at the top of the stairs. I could feel that one leg was useless, and the other didn't hurt as much, so I cautiously used it to propel myself forward, not sure if it would hurt as well. Even now, I can recall every detail: the room's layout, its rough carpet, the landing, the soft blue hue of the carpeted stairs, the freshly painted white ornate balustrade, the wallpaper that covered the stairs, the window looking out on a grey English morning. As I perched at the top of the stairs, I let out piercing cries, praying my mother would hear me from the kitchen, hoping that my brother would come to my rescue - where was he? Why did he desert me when I so needed him? These thoughts crossed my mind, and now, many, many years later, they are just as clear to me as they were then. The pain I felt then is the same pain I feel now in my memory – it has never left me.

Her voice finally echoed up the stairs, a mix of concern and frustration. "I thought I told you not to go upstairs! Why are you crying?" The relief that washed over me was immense; my mother had come to my rescue.

The subsequent events are now a blur, but one thing was certain: in that moment of distress, my mother had been my savior.

For nearly a decade, agony and hope were my constant companions. The cold, sterile hospital rooms became my second home, each visit filling me with hope that I would finally be cured of this horrible bone disease that refused all conventional treatment. I can still feel the sharp pain of the surgeries and the relentless throbbing pain that orthopedic operations brought. Yet, amid this sea of torment, there were islands of warmth and compassion: the gentle hands of the nurses who cared for me, their comforting words whispered during my darkest moments.

During my deepest moments of despair, there was a peaceful place that my adolescent imagination conjured: "angels." These radiant beings, resembling compassionate and kind nurses, became my source of solace. Among them, one remains etched in my memory since the young age of four. I can vividly recall her – she held me aloft, cradling me with her gentle touch after cleansing me and readying me for surgery. I was clad in a pristine white gown; she raised me up. "You are a beautiful angel," she whispered, her voice carrying the weight of tenderness. "God loves you so much." Her face, I remember distinctly, emanated not just beauty but an encompassing warmth that reached the core of my being. To this very day, I still distinctly recall the feeling of peace, love, care, and kindness that she embued in me. She took away my fear and replaced it with the knowledge that everything was perfect.

In my bleakest moments, during the English cold nights when pain surged beyond endurance when I lay alone in the chill of a hospital bed, these celestial figures would grace me with their presence. They enveloped me in a cocoon of comfort, guiding me through the shadows until the agony subsided.

My mother's daily visits were my foundation in those days; her presence was a constant reminder of unconditional love. I would listen for the unique sound her shoes made on the hard floor as she entered the ward. Each evening, no matter how drained from his day in the city of London, my father would be there, a quiet pillar of strength before he journeyed back home. He never missed an evening visit. Every evening, he told me a part of a story that he was making up in his mind. I waited with bated breath for the next installment.

The diagnosis was a very rare bone disease afflicting one specific bone in my leg. This bone, fragile and unable to regenerate as it should, continuously fractured without the ability to mend itself. Surgeons, with their vast expertise, tried every conceivable solution, but the answers eluded them. From the tender age of three until I was twelve, my leg was in a repetitive cycle of breaks and mends, always encased in the confining embrace of a cast or a brace.

I was a spirited boy, eager to keep up with my peers, yet my broken leg often slowed me down. My parents, with their wise and balanced approach, refused to coddle me or offer unnecessary privileges because of my condition. They treated me with the same expectations and standards they held for my siblings, fostering a sense of normalcy and resilience in me. Their greatest gift was the stability they provided—a childhood where I never questioned their unwavering love or support. Their tough-love approach, steady yet compassionate, became the foundation for how I lived my life, teaching me strength, independence, and perseverance.

> *My disability was not a disability; it was an opportunity.*

By the time I reached twelve, the medical discussions veered towards amputation. I eagerly embraced the idea. My only desire was to be like the other kids: to swim, to run, to ride a bike. After heartfelt conversations with my parents and understanding the profound implications, I stood resolute. They consented, and surgeons amputated my leg below the knee.

That decision marked my true awakening to life. With my new prosthetic, I embarked on the journey of relearning basic motions. In merely six months, I was walking and even managing a unique hopping run. I took up cycling and swimming, relishing every moment of my newfound freedom.

Just as before, my parents made no concessions; I was treated exactly like my siblings, and I was expected to participate in all family activities. My disability was not a disability; it was an opportunity to prove that I could do as much or more than anyone else - this is what my parents infused in me from the start, and it is a lesson that has guided me through life to this day.

From then on, there was no looking back. My amputation was not a weight I carried; it sometimes brought pain, but it never felt burdensome. On the contrary, it emerged as a blessing. Unlike some who grieve the loss of a limb, I didn't sink into despair or feel encumbered. I wholeheartedly accepted my path and celebrated every victory. To this day, the simple joys, like walking barefoot on grass, savoring its cool texture - a pleasure I'd missed before the amputation - fill my heart with gratitude.

Elaine

The air outside the Coffee Bean buzzed with the lively energy of Montrose, a sharp contrast to the stillness that settled over me when I spotted Gideon, strolling past without noticing me.

"Gideon," I called out, keeping my tone light even as a knot of nervousness tightened in my chest.

"Oh, there you are!" he said, stopping abruptly. "Sorry, I didn't see you." There was a flicker of embarrassment in his voice.

I couldn't resist teasing him. "How could you not notice me?" I raised an eyebrow, half-serious, half-joking.

He gave me a once-over and shrugged with a small smile. "You look so different from the last time I saw you."

He wasn't wrong. Gone was the polished professional or the yoga-pants traveler he'd met before. Today, it was just me in a T-shirt and ripped jeans—relaxed, unassuming, and unfamiliar to him.

We decided to grab coffee, a gesture that bridged the gap of the moment. Sitting across from each other, surrounded by the hum of the world, the conversation turned to uncharted territory. I suggested friendship, framing it as a safe and steady shore we could both reach for.

But Gideon's response caught me off guard. "No," he said, his voice firm and deliberate. "We can't be friends. It's all or nothing with us. If I can't be close to you, I don't want to see you at all."

His honesty hit hard, peeling back layers I hadn't even realized were there. I could see his feelings, clear as day, but my resolve kicked in. I wasn't just me; I was a pastor, a leader. I had a duty, a path I couldn't veer from, no matter how tempting.

I opened up, sharing the chaos of my life—the looming move, the unraveling of my marriage, and the relentless demands of my calling. It felt raw, like a confession, each word reinforcing why Gideon couldn't be more than a passing figure in this season of my life.

He reached out, placing his hand over mine, his touch warm and steady. "It's all OK," he said softly, his voice calming the storm that was now raging inside of me.

But it was too much. I pulled my hand away, a reflexive move to protect the fragile balance I'd managed to maintain. His touch was a door to vulnerability I wasn't ready to walk through, not with so much at stake.

"Let's take a walk," Gideon suggested, standing up.

The Southern California sun wrapped us in its gentle warmth as we strolled along Honolulu Avenue. The quaint boutiques and lively street brought a sense of normalcy, a welcome distraction. Our conversation stayed light, weaving around the weight of our earlier exchange. It was like we were both trying to ease the transition back to our separate realities.

Then, out of nowhere, Gideon asked, "Did you notice anything about my leg?"

I glanced down, puzzled. For the first time, I really noticed his shorts, exposing his legs. They seemed fine to me. "No," I said, frowning. "What's wrong with it?"

He guided my eyes, pointing out what I'd missed. Finally, I saw it. "Oh... Is one of your legs artificial?" I asked, surprised.

He nodded. "Yes. I lost it years ago. I thought you'd noticed by now that I walk with a limp."

"I didn't," I admitted, marveling at the realistic look of his prosthetic. "It's amazing. Now that you mention it, I do notice a slight limp."

"That's intentional," he said. "I've spent years practicing walking without a limp, but it still shows sometimes, especially when I'm tired."

We eventually returned to our cars, a quiet settling over us like a heavy blanket. It felt like we were at a crossroads, each standing on the edge of a decision we weren't quite ready to make. His eyes held something unspoken, a sadness that matched the ache in my chest.

Without a word, Gideon got in his car. I stood there, watching as he drove away, the sound of his departure leaving a void in its wake. The moment lingered, full of everything that could have been but wouldn't be, as I turned and walked back into the life I'd chosen.

I was frozen in my car, my heart racing, every emotion crashing over me like tumultuous waves. Every fiber of my being was resonating with the intensity of what I had just realized at this moment. I had arrived with the intent to sever a bond that had just begun to form, a task that should've been simple. Everything had gone exactly according to plan until that one unexpected revelation, which now left me reeling.

"Why did he draw my attention to his leg?" I pondered, my breath uneven. The weight of recognition pressed heavily on me as I connected the dots, sending shivers racing across my skin. "How could this be real?"

In 1994, I stood at a crossroads, staring at the gates of the seminary, far from the comforts of my Hawaiian home. Los Angeles, bustling and impersonal, became my new reality—a city where no one knew my name. Full-time ministry had never been part of my plan, but somehow, a divine nudge propelled me toward graduate school. With college behind me, I had envisioned a different future, one where I'd follow the life I thought I wanted.

Then, I met him. A man whose accomplishments seemed to align perfectly with my own ambitions. Freshly armed with a Ph.D., he was on the cusp of a promising career in academia and politics back in Korea. Everything about him checked the boxes: an esteemed family, an exceptional education, a commanding presence, and impeccable manners. Though he didn't share my Christian faith, I believed he was the one. When I introduced him to my parents as my future husband, my father—who has an extraordinary gift for reading people—saw his potential and eventually gave us his blessing.

A trip to Korea, however, unveiled the weight of tradition and expectations. As the eldest son, my fiancé faced pressure to marry quickly. His family wanted a March wedding, and they wanted it soon. But this clashed with my family's reality. My parents, already stretched thin financially, were in the midst of planning my sister's wedding. They couldn't shoulder the burden of two weddings back-to-back.

When I returned home, the practicalities of our situation became impossible to ignore. I knew I had to step in. I asked my fiancé and his family for a delay—a little time to gather resources and plan a wedding that felt right for everyone. What happened next blindsided me.

He disappeared. Calls went unanswered, messages ignored, and the life we had started building together crumbled in silence. The man I thought I'd marry was gone, and with him, the future I had envisioned.

As I grappled with heartbreak, my dreams began to speak. In one vivid dream, I ran to my fiancé with hope in my heart, only to be stopped by a yawning chasm. I fell into its depths, my cries swallowed by silence. In another, I was dressed in a wedding gown, but without a veil, as though something essential was missing. The scene shifted, and I found myself clothed in clerical robes, standing amidst garments that seemed to represent my calling—one I hadn't yet embraced.

These dreams continued during my time at the seminary, each one peeling back layers of divine intention. One, in particular, stood out. I was with a husband, a man who walked with a pronounced limp. We lived in a home with a central courtyard—a peaceful sanctuary unlike anything I'd known. That dream lingered, especially in light of my recent encounter with Gideon.

The symbolism of the limp felt profound, like a marker of shared resilience. It hinted at a journey not yet revealed, one where my path might intertwine with someone shaped by life's trials but fortified by them. The dreams, the divine whispers, and even my heartbreak seemed to converge, pointing me toward a future I couldn't yet fully grasp.

The next morning, I sheepishly sent Gideon a simple text message.

> Good morning. Wishing you a wonderful day!

>> You too

>> Btw. You can call me if you have time and want to.

Gideon and I were set on a specific path defined by the Devine, it was a path that was choreographed from our first breaths. Despite the turns and twirls of life, The Divine ensured we would meet. Even when I hesitated, The Divine nudged me back onto the destined path. Gideon's journey, marked by the necessary loss of a leg, was never one of lament. Instead, it was a testament to resilience and grace. It was as if God made his life easier. In the challenges, he found strength, in adversity, an abundance of blessings.

God placed his soul with the perfect family. They provided him with everything he needed to survive the loss of a leg and not view it as a disability but rather as an opportunity. They provided him with the strength that was required to reach that serendipitous moment when I waivered and the divine plan was in danger.

"Look at my leg, look at it, look carefully," he had implored of me. I did, and it changed everything.

The Divine purpose behind our union remains a beautiful enigma. Perhaps we're key players in a story much larger than ourselves, or perhaps mere pawns set to play a limited role. Reflecting on life's myriad moments, we can only glimpse hints of this greater plan.

There's an orchestration to existence, a symphony we're all a part of. While some might have fleeting solos, others carry the melody longer. Recognizing the divine touch in our lives, it's essential to heed those subtle nudges, the cosmic whispers guiding us. They place us precisely where we need to be, aligning us with the grand vision The Divine has mapped out for us all.

Chapter Twelve

Death

It is not death that a man should fear, but he should fear never beginning to live. - Marcus Aurelius

How will you evaluate your existence when you find yourself on the threshold of death? As you arrive at your final moment, your ultimate reflection, how will you sum up the life you've led? Will you look back upon a life brimming with purpose? Will you recollect a life devoted to serving others? Will there be a tinge of regret for the countless hours spent toiling away at work? What will be the testament of your life?

The immortal soul, eager for the liberation that accompanies the body's demise, faces a bittersweet moment. The day of freedom is also a day of loss, a severing from its spiritual counterpart. The remaining spirituality within the immortal soul is largely dependent on the life one has led. For some, death ushers in peace and the comforting knowledge of the soul's eternal continuation. For others, it is a time filled with regret.

Imagine yourself standing on the edge of death, feeling the life ebbing from your mortal soul while your immortal soul begins to stir, preparing to leave its earthly vessel. In that moment, with the veil of life lifting, the distinct roles of these two souls become uncomfortably clear. What would you see as the sum of your life's choices and accomplishments?

If your mortal soul—the part driven by fleeting pleasures, material gains, and self-centered desires—held sway during your life, its imminent extinction might bring an unbearable sense of emptiness. All that once seemed so essential—your possessions, status, and worldly pursuits—would crumble into insignificance. The joy they once provided now feels hollow, their worth dissolving as your mortal soul fades into nothingness. You might wonder, "Was it all wasted?"

But if your immortal soul—the part connected to the eternal, the divine, and the pursuit of higher purpose—guided your life's course, the view is vastly different. In the face of death, you may feel a deep sense of peace, knowing that your existence was not squandered on what cannot endure. You built something lasting, not with brick and mortar, but with love, virtue, and spiritual enrichment. Your mortal life nourished your immortal soul, preparing it for eternity.

This shift in perspective is stark, for death does not negotiate. It strips away the layers of our mortal concerns, revealing what truly mattered. The most cherished possessions we clung to, the careers we tirelessly pursued, and even the physical health we so often prioritized—all are left behind. What transcends is the immortal soul, carrying with it the legacy of how we chose to live.

At the threshold of death, clarity sharpens. If we lived primarily for the mortal soul, chasing desires and neglecting our divine purpose, regret may wash over us. Time spent hoarding wealth or prioritizing ambition over love and connection becomes a haunting reminder of misaligned priorities. However, if we embraced our immortal soul—cultivating kindness, seeking truth, and living for others—our final moments may reveal a life well lived, brimming with eternal significance.

Death, in its inevitability, teaches us the ultimate truth: what we feed and nurture during our lives—our mortal desires or our immortal purpose—determines how we view our existence when it reaches its end. Choose wisely, for this decision echoes into eternity.

The Fear of Death

Death is the great equalizer, a threshold that every living being will eventually cross. Whether it comes swiftly or gives us time to prepare, it lays bare the choices we've made and the priorities we've lived by. For many, the approach of death stirs fear—particularly for those whose lives were spent indulging the demands of the mortal soul. This part of us, tied to our physical existence, is concerned solely with survival, comfort, and fleeting pleasures. Its extinction at death is inevitable, and to accept this is to confront its deepest fear: the end of its existence.

Those who have lived primarily for their mortal soul, chasing material gain, status, or physical gratification, often find themselves gripped by this fear. Death threatens everything they have valued, for their pursuits were tied to the transient world. The mortal soul, which cannot imagine a purpose beyond its own survival, fills their final moments with dread. Its resistance to death is not out of malice, but simply because it was never designed to transcend.

In contrast, there are those who have nurtured their immortal soul—the eternal essence that connects us to the divine and the infinite. These individuals have chosen to prioritize spiritual growth, selflessness, and the cultivation of love, gratitude, and joy. They understand that the immortal soul does not perish with the body but instead returns to its divine origin, enriched by the wisdom and experiences gathered in this life.

For these individuals, death holds no terror. Their lives have been lived in alignment with their higher purpose, and they approach the end with peace and a sense of accomplishment. Having invested in what truly matters—acts of kindness, the pursuit of truth, and the betterment of the world—they harbor no regrets. They see their earthly journey as complete, a contribution to humanity and an offering to the divine.

As their mortal bodies fade, their immortal souls stand ready, fortified by the spiritual treasures they have accumulated. To them, death is not an end but a transition—a moment of release into the infinite. These souls embrace death as a homecoming, a return to the source of all love and life. They face it not with fear, but with gratitude for the life they've lived and anticipation for what lies beyond.

In the end, the way we approach death mirrors the way we lived. Those who have fed their immortal soul with the riches of spirit—compassion, gratitude, and selfless love—find that the threshold of death is not a boundary to be feared, but a gateway to eternal peace.

The Moment of Death

Some years ago, I met a hospice nurse whose work brought her closer to the reality of death than most of us ever experience. She carried countless stories, each shaped by the fragility and beauty of life's final moments. Compassionate and deeply committed, she dedicated herself to helping her patients and their families navigate the transition from life to death. One of her stories stayed with me, not just for its poignancy, but for the profound truth it revealed.

She shared the tale of an elderly man, gripped by an overwhelming fear of death. Despite her best efforts, his dread was unshakable, a shadow she couldn't lift. After doing all she could to comfort him, she left him in the care of his caregiver and headed home. As she sat in her car, preparing to leave, something extraordinary happened. She suddenly felt his voice in her mind—calm and awestruck—describing the beauty of what he was experiencing. He spoke of regret, not for the life he was leaving, but for not realizing sooner how wonderful this transition would be. Moments later, her phone rang. The caregiver was calling to inform her the man had passed.

The nurse believed, and I do too, that such encounters speak to the joy the immortal soul experiences upon its release. For a lifetime, the immortal soul remains confined within the human body, bound by the demands of the mortal soul. But as death approaches, the mortal soul weakens, its influence over the body fading. This moment is the immortal soul's time to rise, stepping into its role and leading the individual into an existence beyond imagination.

Those who have spent their lives nurturing their immortal soul often greet this moment with a sense of peace and familiarity. Their spiritual practices and selfless acts have prepared them for what lies beyond. For others, who've lived in service to the mortal soul—pursuing material gain, indulgence, or self-interest—there is often regret. In their final moments, they glimpse life's true purpose, only to realize too late how far they strayed from it.

As the mortal soul relinquishes control, many find themselves experiencing vivid visions of loved ones who have passed. These are not physical forms but spiritual presences, revealed through the lens of the immortal soul. It is a reunion, a homecoming, as the dying person is welcomed by companions from the spiritual realm. This joyous encounter is a profound affirmation of the soul's eternal nature.

However, the transition isn't always serene. For those steeped in negativity or consumed by evil during their lives, the immortal soul may be too weakened to assert itself. In such cases, the dying person clings to their basest instincts until their final breath, unable to experience the release and joy that others do.

For most, though, the immortal soul shines as the mortal soul fades. Compassion, love, and even regret may sweep over them—a flood of emotions from the soul now freed from its earthly constraints. Yet, no matter how profound this realization, it comes too late to change a life already lived.

Death is the mortal soul's end and the body's final farewell. What remains of our earthly presence is a legacy—a memory that, too, will fade with time. But the immortal soul carries on, jubilant in its liberation. Its state, however, depends entirely on how it was nurtured during its time on Earth. Whether it ascends full of joy or weighed down by neglect is determined by the priorities we chose to embrace in life. In this way, death is not just an end—it is the culmination of how we lived, a mirror reflecting the truth of our choices.

The physical body, once vibrant and animated by the spiritual soul and spirit, begins to deteriorate almost immediately after death. Its rapid decay is a stark reminder of the body's transient nature and dependency on the spiritual essence that once inhabited it. We honor the body not for what it becomes in death, but for the sacred role it played in housing a soul—a fragment of the Divine—during its earthly journey.

When the spiritual soul departs, it is instinctively repelled by the decaying flesh and moves swiftly toward the realm of souls, its true home. This separation marks the end of life as we know it, underscoring the profound connection between the spirit and the body. While the spirit remains, the body is a vessel of life; the moment it departs, the process of decay is inevitable and immediate.

Cultural and religious practices surrounding the treatment of the body after death reflect varying beliefs about its sanctity and the transition of the soul. In many Eastern traditions, cremation is performed as quickly as possible, signifying a release of the soul and a return to the natural cycle. In contrast, Western religious practices often favor burial, though cremation has also become widely accepted over time.

Judaism, particularly in its orthodox traditions, emphasizes the importance of burying the body as soon as possible, in keeping with the belief that the body is inherently sacred[1] . It is seen as a vessel that partnered with the soul in fulfilling divine commandments and is therefore treated with the utmost

---

1. There is a large body of Jewish literature that deals extensively with the burial of the dead. In Genesis (3:19), God declares of man: "For dust you are, and to dust you shall return."Deuteronomy (21:23) commands in the case of an executed criminal, "You shall surely bury him." The requirement of burying the dead is explicitly codified in many multiple later rabbinic sources as well, including The Talmud (Sanhedrin 46b), and Maimonides' Sefer Hamitzvot, as well as the Shulchan Aruch - Code of Jewish Law.

respect. Cremation, in this context, is considered a desecration of the body, as it interrupts the traditional burial process meant to honor its sanctity.

Across all traditions, these practices underscore a shared reverence for the body as more than just a physical entity. It is remembered as a temporary home for the divine spark, a tangible reminder of the soul's earthly journey and its ultimate destination beyond this life.

Why No One Comes Back

Although there are instances where a mortal soul might linger momentarily after death, this is not a universal occurrence. A soul that remains in this world is out of its natural element; it cannot sustain its existence here and has no desire to. Having broken free from the human body's confinement, it is primed to return to its rightful place. The soul recognizes this destination, a spiritual sanctuary, and is free to journey back to it. There have been stories suggesting that sometimes, the soul remains tied to living bodies due to deep connections with other souls. However, it's important to understand that such instances typically occur when two immortal souls have intimately bonded, reflecting those individuals who have nurtured their immortal souls and allowed them to guide their consciousness.

Our fascination with the spectral world often leads us to weave tales of ghosts, perhaps as a means of reassuring ourselves of an existence beyond death. Regardless of whether these stories are intended to incite fear or comfort us with the belief in an afterlife, narratives of ghostly encounters permeate virtually every culture. [2] (Brodt, 2020) A renowned example features Abraham Lincoln, whom many claim to have encountered within the confines of the White House.

Winston Churchill, the British Prime Minister during World War II, is known to have had a unique experience with the supposed ghost of Abraham Lincoln during his stay at the White House. According to the anecdote, Churchill was staying in the Lincoln Bedroom, which is said to be one of the most haunted rooms in the White House.

The story goes that after a long day of work and discussions with President Franklin D. Roosevelt, Churchill decided to take a hot bath to unwind. He was known for enjoying baths with a cigar and a glass of scotch. As he emerged from the bathroom, naked with the cigar in his mouth, he walked into the bedroom to find the apparition of President Lincoln standing by the fireplace, seemingly deep in thought.

Churchill, not one to be easily frightened or flustered, reportedly said, "Good evening, Mr. President. You seem to have me at a disadvantage." The ghost of Lincoln then smiled and vanished into thin air, leaving Churchill alone in the room.

---

2. https://boundarystones.weta.org/2020/10/29/legends
   -lincolns-ghost

This encounter is just one of many reported sightings of Abraham Lincoln's ghost in the White House, adding to the lore surrounding one of the world's most iconic and historic residences. Others who are attributed with seeing Lincoln's ghost include First Lady Grace Coolidge and Queen Wilhelmina of the Netherlands, as well as many staff and other temporary residents of the White House.

Although it is possible for souls to linger in the earthly realm, such occurrences are rare and potentially distressing for the soul.

When the soul departs the body, it swiftly returns to its origin, unshackled and free to embrace its true spiritual nature. As a being of pure spirit, the soul has no attachment to the physical world or the body it temporarily inhabited. Its time in the human realm was one of reluctant confinement, a spiritual essence bound to a perishable vessel of flesh. This mismatch of essence and form can feel burdensome, even torturous, as the soul struggles to fully express its divine qualities within the limitations of the physical world. Upon release, it finds liberation, returning to a realm of divine light and perfect harmony, where it rejoices in peace and contentment among kindred souls.

The soul's true home is a realm untouched by time or space as we understand them. What we experience as a lifetime is but a fleeting moment in the spiritual dimension. The Higher Power, unbound by temporal and spatial constraints, sees all—past, present, and future—as a singular, eternal reality. In this timeless existence, the soul is immersed in the fullness of its divine purpose.

Disturbing the Soul

While it is theoretically possible for a soul to manifest again in the mortal realm, there is no desire to do so. The soul, once liberated, perceives the human world as harsh and limiting compared to its native state. Attempts to summon a soul back through rituals such as séances are not only unnecessary but also disruptive and selfish. These rituals often stem from the living's need for closure or answers, but they can be deeply unsettling for the soul, which has no interest in mundane human concerns once it has returned to the spiritual realm.

Séances, in particular, are a human invention driven by the desire to bridge the gap between life and death. Participants join hands, often in dimly lit rooms, guided by a medium who claims to channel spirits. While many believe they have successfully communicated with the dead, these experiences are typically anecdotal and influenced by psychological factors such as suggestion, emotional need, or the collective dynamics of the group. The lack of scientific evidence further underscores the ambiguous nature of these encounters.

Even if such rituals were to succeed in reaching a soul, it is unlikely to yield meaningful results. The soul exists in a realm where human concerns—time, space, and material possessions—are irrelevant. Asking a soul to engage with the human world again, even briefly, can be distressing and disorienting for it. The act itself reflects a human-centric perspective, often disregarding the soul's peace and fulfillment in its spiritual abode.

Ultimately, the desire to connect with the departed must be tempered by respect for the soul's journey. Rather than attempting to draw it back into a world, it has left behind, we should honor its transition by embracing our own spiritual growth and preparing ourselves for the day when we, too, will return to the realm of the eternal. In doing so, we align with the divine order, fostering peace for both the living and the departed.

Death, a New Beginning

Rather than fearing death as a grim inevitability, we should see it as the natural conclusion of our earthly journey—a transition we can prepare for through lives devoted to spiritual growth and purpose. By embracing and practicing spiritual values, we align ourselves with the soul's higher calling. This alignment brings fulfillment and peace, allowing us to view death not as a loss but as a homecoming—a return to the eternal realm, often referred to as heaven.

Death is not a punishment or an end; it is a liberation. It frees the immortal soul from the confines of the physical body, which, though necessary for earthly life, often feels like a prison to the spiritual soul. Imagine a bird, caged and longing to stretch its wings, finally released into the boundless sky. Such is the soul's release at death—a freedom from the limitations, decay, and mortal concerns of the human body.

> *As we grow spiritual-*
> *ly, our immortal soul*
> *strengthens and evolves.*

During life, the spiritual soul often wrestles with the dominance of the mortal soul—a self-centered, survival-driven force that pulls us toward materialism, indulgence, and selfishness. This struggle can feel like a form of hell for the spiritual soul, whose essence is purity, love, and connection to the divine. Yet, death unshackles the spiritual soul, allowing it to return to its true home, where it rejoices in the warmth of divine light and the companionship of other souls.

Our understanding of concepts like heaven, hell, good, and evil has been shaped over millennia by mythology and religious interpretations, often molded to fit specific narratives. But the soul itself transcends religion. It is unconcerned with dogmas or rituals; its sole focus is spirituality—growing, achieving purity, and reuniting with the divine spiritual realm.

When we strip away religious constructs and focus on the soul's intrinsic mission, our earthly purpose becomes clearer: to overcome the mortal soul's selfish inclinations and contribute to the betterment of humanity. This work is not about adhering to specific doctrines but about fostering love, compassion, and harmony—creating a world where the divine presence could dwell among us.

> *The soul itself transcends religion. It is unconcerned with dogmas or rituals.*

As we grow spiritually, our immortal soul strengthens and evolves. The mission of the immortal soul during its time on Earth is to leave this life in a higher state of spirituality than when it entered. It is through acts of selflessness, kindness, and a dedication to the greater good that we achieve this transformation.

On the day we die, the state of our soul reflects how we have lived. A soul enriched by spiritual growth will leave the body invigorated, ready to soar into the infinite with a greater connection to the divine. This is the ultimate purpose of our earthly existence: to nurture the immortal soul, so that it may fulfill its divine destiny beyond the physical realm.

Chapter Thirteen

What Does God Care About?

Where mercy, love, and pity dwell, there God is dwelling too. -
William Blake

Religion, in essence, outlines what a Higher Power expects of us, particularly in the case of the three major faiths, which primarily draw upon the Bible or the Quran. However, the Bible's vast scope for various interpretations often leads to diverging perspectives within the same religion despite referencing the same verse. The presence of contradictory verses further complicates this issue, fostering debates over which law supersedes another. The doctrine of a religion is essentially a particular denomination's interpretation of the Bible. Yet, most mainstream religions, setting aside extreme ideologies, concur that reaching heaven requires being a moral individual, respectful of others, and refraining from deceit, theft, or crime. Additional stipulations vary by religion, such as upholding the commandments of the Torah in Judaism or recognizing Jesus as your savior in Christianity.

While the Bible serves as a valuable starting point to comprehend divine will, detailing the relationship between humankind and The Higher Power, it may not suffice for an in-depth understanding. This comprehension necessitates viewing the matter from a different perspective.

We must analyze the relationship between the soul and The Divine to discern what God desires. Examining this connection from the viewpoint of the soul provides a fresh insight into God's true concerns. Throughout this book, we've persistently viewed life from the dual-soul perspective. But to decipher God's true intent, we must set aside the mortal animalistic soul and focus exclusively on the immortal, spiritual one. The mortal soul lacks the required spirituality; by nature, it is only concerned with the temporary earthly experience; it has no direct connection with The Higher Power and shows little to no interest in the spiritual realm. Only through the immortal spiritual soul that contains a sliver of The Divine can we begin to comprehend God's expectations and concerns.

A cursory reading of the Torah offers a certain degree of understanding regarding the divine will. Delving into the interpretations of the Torah can take us further. Yet, it may not provide a comprehensive grasp of the divine will from a spiritual viewpoint. When we read the Torah and apply the notions of a sacred, immortal soul and an impure, mortal soul to the commandments and narrative, their meanings become more transparent, sometimes reinforcing the message or clarifying otherwise perplexing commandments or narratives.

The Zohar, the mystic commentary on the Torah, is part of a Jewish mystical tradition known as Kabbalah. It offers extensive insight into the relationship between The Divine and humanity, the origins of the cosmos, and various other topics. However, its rich symbolism and complexity can make it hard to decipher. Although originally written in Aramaic, it has been translated into English, yet its understanding may still require a teacher's guidance.

When we approach traditional texts from a soul-first perspective, the deep meaning of these texts evolve and sometimes can take on a totally different meaning.

One of the holiest prayers in Judaism, a prayer that is mentioned twice a day, every day by observant Jews, is" the Shema" (the word *"Shema"* means "hear" and is taken from the first word of the prayer) found in Deuteronomy 6:4-9:

> *"Hear, O Israel: The Lord is our God, the Lord is one. **You shall love the Lord your God with all your heart, and with all your soul, and with all your might.** Keep these words that I am commanding you today in your heart..."*
>
> Deuteronomy 6:4-9

"You shall love the Lord your God with all your heart, with all your soul, and with all your might." This statement is frequently echoed by Christians, Jews, and Muslims, embodying an ultimate affirmation of faith. Nonetheless, I've found these words somewhat unsettling as the literal interpretation seemed to miss the mark. We are indeed commanded to love our God, but how does one mandate an emotion like love? Yes, it's possible to make a commitment to love, which is probably how most people interpret this passage. However, I would like to examine this passage from a different perspective – a soul-first perspective. In the mortal realm, any attempts to command love typically result in the opposite effect, creating distance instead of closeness, for love is an emotion that evolves into a commitment, not a directive. Wouldn't it be more reasonable for God to say, "Know me, and then you will love me, and then you will commit to me?" That could align with human logic but not necessarily with the soul's perspective.

Approaching this statement from the viewpoint of the soul begins to decipher the beautifully layered intent of the sentence. Here, we encounter four key elements: God, the Heart, the Soul, and our Strength. Intriguingly, they all interconnect. God is represented by our spirit. The soul symbolizes our internal immortal spiritual entity; the heart, devoid of emotions any more than our lungs or kidneys, signifies the body; our might implies the necessary strength to execute this commandment. Here, The Higher Power, God, invites us to fill our bodies with the soul's attribute of love, as love originates from the spirit embedded in the soul. This process requires all our might to subdue the mortal soul's selfish impulses represented by the body. We must strive for a state where our immortal spiritual soul transcends the animalistic mortal soul, imbuing us with divine attributes and, most importantly – love. After accomplishing this, we will comprehend God, embody the spirit at its highest level, and accomplish God's plan for attaining the ultimate spiritual state. This understanding brings clarity to the rest of the *Shema* verses, allowing us to view them through the soul's lens and reinforcing this interpretation.

Scripture offers countless clues and interpretations regarding God's expectations. However, to discern what truly matters to God, we need to explore the closest earthly embodiment of The Divine - our immortal soul. This spiritual part of us accompanies us throughout our lives. Yet, many of us rarely attempt to comprehend its nature and demands. Ironically, many spend their entire lives in pursuit of God, unaware that the divine resides within us. Rather than gazing upward, we need to direct our attention inward, for it is within our souls that we encounter the divine.

We have spoken much about what the immortal soul requires of us in order to grow spiritually. It is clear that positive interactions with other souls and positive interactions with God's creations enable the soul to increase its spirituality so that it may reach a level that enables it to be one with The Divine. God created humans in Their image, giving humans Their divine attributes. What are God's attributes? We can learn a lot about them from the immortal soul, and in addition, they are listed in the bible many times; for instance, in Exodus, we find a list of them:

> *(6) The LORD passed before him and proclaimed: "The LORD! the LORD! a God **compassionate** and **gracious**, **slow to anger**, abounding in **kindness** and **faithfulness**, (7) **extending kindness** to the thousandth generation, **forgiving** iniquity, transgression, and sin —yet not remitting all punishment, but visiting the iniquity of parents upon children and children's children, upon the third and fourth generations."*
>
> Exodus 34: 6 - 7

Examining the soul's perspective and drawing upon biblical references, it becomes evident that God's characteristics are overwhelmingly positive: kindness, forgiveness, compassion, and love. These are the attributes that They expect us to embody, and these are the very qualities They imbued us with when They created us in "Their likeness." These attributes, indeed, mirror the image of God.

Up until now, it is clear that God seeks these attributes in humans—qualities intrinsic to the immortal spiritual soul. But there is more to this understanding. Greater insight can be found in the Torah, specifically in Leviticus chapter 19. This chapter begins with the following words:

> *Speak to the whole Israelite community and say to them: You shall be holy, for I, the Lord your God am holy.*

Leviticus 19

The chapter then continues to list a long list of civil commands, for instance:

- "'Do not steal."

- "'Do not lie."

- "'Do not deceive one another."

- "'Do not swear falsely by my name and so profane the name of your God. I am the Lord."

- "'Do not defraud or rob your neighbor."

- "'Do not hold back the wages of a hired worker overnight."

- "'Do not pervert justice; do not show partiality to the poor or favoritism to the great, but judge your neighbor fairly."

- "'Do not go about spreading slander among your people."

- "'Do not do anything that endangers your neighbor's life. I am the Lord."

- "'Do not hate a fellow Israelite in your heart. Rebuke your neighbor frankly so you will not share in their guilt."

- "'Do not seek revenge or bear a grudge against anyone among your people, but **love your neighbor as yourself**. I am the Lord."

Unmistakably, the list encapsulates the mandate to love your neighbor as yourself—a foundation of all commandments and the three Abrahamic religions. God implores us to emulate Their sanctity and immediately presents us with a set of commandments — ingredients for justice that underpin civil law across the globe. They are instructing us to live our lives as they do, imbued with love, kindness, forgiveness, and compassion. It's a blueprint for a world escalating in spirituality, differentiating itself from the animal kingdom—a world reflecting The Higher Power's qualities and those of the immortal soul.

Compassion, Mercy, and Punishment

Unambiguously, The Higher Power invites us to build a world where They can feel at home—a place where spiritual souls can coexist. They're calling upon humanity to perfect the world They've initiated as their co-creators.

In the same verse, Exodus 34: 6 - 7, we not only read a list of God's positive attributes, but we also see an additional attribute that seemingly doesn't quite fit into the list. Along with attributes such as compassion, kindness, faithfulness, forgiveness, etc., we are also introduced to Their attribute of justice as in:

> "... yet not remitting all **punishment**, but visiting the **iniquity** of parents upon children and children's children, upon the third and fourth generations."
>
> Exodus 34: 6 - 7

The emphasis God places on justice, alongside compassion, mercy, and kindness, is both intriguing and significant. It suggests that for a harmonious world, mere compassion isn't sufficient; the element of justice is crucial to maintaining equilibrium for mankind.

In a study titled "Divergent Effects of Beliefs in Heaven and Hell on National Crime Rates," [1] (Shariff, 2012), Shariff and Rhemtulla discovered an intriguing trend: societies that pre-

---

1. Shariff, A., & Rhemtulla, M. (2012). Divergent effects of beliefs in heaven and hell on national crime rates. PLOS ONE, 7(6), e39048. https://doi.org/10.1371/journal.po ne.0039048

dominantly believed in heaven had increased crime rates. In contrast, those with a more pronounced belief in hell showed decreased crime incidents. This pattern persisted regardless of religious affiliations, national origins, or socio-economic backgrounds.

In the study, they state:

> *"Human monitors cannot see all transgressions, human judgers cannot adjudicate with perfect precision, and human punishers are neither able to apprehend every transgressor, nor escape the potential dangers of retribution. Divine punishment, on the other hand, has emerged as a cultural tool to overcome a number of those limitations. Unlike humans, divine punishers can be omniscient, omnipotent, infallible, and untouchable and therefore able to effectively deter transgressors who may for whatever reason be undeterred by earthly policing systems."*
>
> Shariff, 2012

Shariff and Rhemtulla's findings align with what God told Moses and is articulated so clearly in Exodus Chapter 4:6-7. Here, as in numerous studies, the message is clear: mercy and compassion alone cannot lay the foundation for a society; justice is equally indispensable. A belief in divine repercussions for misdeeds cultivates a society that's not only more forgiving but also inherently spiritual.

God recognized the mortal inclination to deceit when tempted. Driven by greed and self-preservation, attributes associated with the mortal animalistic soul, individuals might exploit communal resources covertly. The notion of divine retribution serves as a deterrent to such dishonest impulses, instilling a sense of moral restraint; one might escape human detection, but not the omniscient Divine. When community welfare is undermined by nepotism or favoritism, the entire society bears the brunt, a sentiment often reflected in the actions of governments and large corporations but originating with individuals.

Holding a belief in divine retribution often fosters forgiveness, with individuals entrusting ultimate justice to God. Conversely, in its absence, societies might gravitate towards punitive measures, extracting a heavy toll on both the wrongdoer and the community at large.

To cultivate a spiritual society, it is incumbent on us to restrain the urges of the mortal animalistic soul with all our might. Though societal laws are vital, we must acknowledge that our unseen personal transgressions not only impact our immortal spiritual souls but also ripple throughout the broader community. Indeed, the Divine is privy to these covert transgressions, as this divine spirit resides within us all. While I don't endorse the concept of hell, I firmly believe that such transgressions negatively impact our immortal souls, creating a spiritual deficit for our souls.

The God and Religion Paradox

God values a civil society where respect for all is the norm—a world where the mortal soul's negative impulses are subdued, compassion, positivity, justice, and kindness preside, a world where love triumphs over hate. God provides a comprehensive guide on how to live a life that will uplift our immortal soul and eradicate the negativity and self-centeredness of the animalistic mortal soul. They're guiding us on how to reconstruct the unique state of the Garden of Eden.

God doesn't limit this task to Jews, Christians, Muslims, whites, or blacks—They show no bias. In the Bible, God instructs the Israelites to pioneer a path forward and exemplify a moral life. While They urge them to be a model to the world, these commandments are not solely for the Israelites; they are not exclusively Jewish—everyone, everywhere, can partner with God in creation to construct a perfect world for Them and the soul.

My wife, Elaine, tells the following narrative: this exchange happened when I first met her on the plane from Seattle to Burbank.

"I don't believe in God. And by the way, I'm Jewish. Do you think non-believers like me, who don't see Jesus as their savior, are destined for hell?" Gideon asked; his question took me by surprise.

Reflecting on my spiritual journey, I responded, "Years ago, I would've said yes. But my beliefs have evolved, and I don't think that way anymore."

"As the years progressed, I found myself entrusted with roles in diverse churches, far removed from the Korean conservative tenets I grew up with, a revolution sparked within my soul. I was fortunate to cross paths with brilliant minds, and enlightened souls who challenged the theological edicts I had always regarded as sacrosanct. I discovered luminous souls, ones who touched lives, radiating kindness and compassion, yet did not recognize Jesus as their savior. How, I grappled, could a benevolent God cast these , beautiful souls, beacons of light into the shadows for their lack of belief in His son? This seismic shift from staunch conservative beliefs to a more embracing theology did not wane my faith. On the contrary, it ignited a fervor, a deeper connection with Jesus, as I felt I was truly tracing His footsteps, unearthing profound truths that lay beneath the surface."

When fate orchestrated our encounter on that plane, and the enigmatic man seated in seat 6A posed that unexpected question, my heart and mind were in the throes of spiritual evolution. I had begun to dive deep into the ancient verses of the Old Testament, seeking the threads that wove it seamlessly with the New. I was enchanted by God's chosen, His firstborn, yearning to fathom the depth of their devotion. It felt like the stars aligned, ushering in Gideon from seat 6A, precisely at this pivotal juncture of my spiritual odyssey.

> *The practice of religion is*
> *the journey; it isn't the*
> *destination itself.*

It's nearly unimaginable to assert that God doesn't concern Themselves with religion; Their focus lies solely on the outcome. They've provided a roadmap for achieving sanctity, which means becoming God-like and merging your spiritual soul with The Divine. Just as they offered the Israelites a roadmap to holiness, other religions have adopted the essentials of that roadmap and discovered their path to spiritual growth. Religion provides the roadmap that leads to a destination of holiness through the spiritual maturation of the immortal soul. The practice of religion is the journey; it isn't the destination itself. God cares about the destination and how each person arrives at that spiritual terminus. Much of what religion has become is preoccupied with the journey rather than the destination. Many religions overly focus on their rituals, forgetting that observance doesn't equate to spirituality. While religious practices and traditions are necessary to sustain religion, when they become the sole reason for religion, its followers become fixated on those aspects, losing sight of the ultimate goal—enhancing the spirituality of the immortal soul and finding holiness with the divine.

Much of what religion has evolved into centers around the practice, its rituals, prayers, and beliefs. However, for many "religious" people, too little of religion focuses on the path that God has explicitly laid out—the path of kindness, compassion, equality, justice for all, and forgiveness, all reflecting God's attributes. Too many religions have declared their path as the only way to salvation—only their followers will be saved. Those who don't share their beliefs are deemed sinners, destined for damnation. Thus, I ask you: How could a Higher Power, embodying compassion, love, and forgiveness for all of their creation, cast aside a soul—perhaps a profoundly righteous soul—for not subscribing to a particular belief? These are not actions of a compassionate and loving God.

> *Religious observance doesn't equate to spirituality.*

God doesn't concern Themselves with religion; They care that religions guide their followers down a path that leads their immortal souls to spiritual growth and, ultimately, unity with The Divine.

God doesn't care about your skin color, nationality, or sexual identity; these mortal traits do not exist in spirituality. God, The Higher Power, They are concerned with your spiritual soul and its spiritual growth. They intended the Garden of Eden to be a unique state where souls could spiritually evolve by interacting with Their creation through Their eyes—by experiencing their positive attributes. Now, it is humanity's task to restore what was destroyed, achievable only by emulating God's qualities and seeing Their creation through Their eyes, for we were created in their likeness. The immortal soul mirrors God's qualities and offers guidance on how to achieve this. God has provided a roadmap and teachings on enhancing the spirituality of the immortal soul; we need only follow that roadmap to reach its prescribed destination.

> *God doesn't care about*
> *your skin color, nation-*
> *ality, or sexual identity.*

When we wield religion to marginalize and oppress others, it ceases to be a path to spiritual growth; instead, it becomes a route to augment the mortal, selfish soul. When we discriminate against the LGBTQI+ communities in God's name, we act out of hate and division—these aren't God's attributes. When we discriminate against other religions and faiths, we disregard those people's immortal, spiritual souls; we act selfishly—an attribute not associated with God. When we use religion to justify marginalizing minorities, black people, Latino people, the poor, women, and orphans, we cater to the mortal soul. God cherishes the [2] oppressed, the widow, the orphan, and those without a voice. Hatred, discrimination, divisiveness, and selfishness are attributes of the mortal soul that will perish with our bodies; they bear no relation to God. Religions that lead their followers down this path steer them away from spiritual growth and from The Divine. Those who tread the path of the mortal soul are no longer a manifestation of the divine image—they have devolved into a manifestation of the mortal animalistic soul.

What does God ultimately want from us? They desire us to reflect Their divine attributes, to become as holy and spiritual as They are. They wish for us to imbue our human consciousness with love. They wish for us to achieve this by establishing a just and civil society, and They've given us the blueprint for it. Ultimately, They wish for us to spiritually grow so that we may become one with The Divine presence—a goal not only for a select group but for all of humanity. God yearns for us to recreate the state of the Garden of Eden—a place where we are judged not by our physical appearances but by the state of our spiritual souls. They desire us to be Their partners in recreating this state of being here on earth.

---

2. Exodus 22:22-23: "Do not take advantage of the widow or the fatherless. If you do and they cry out to me, I will certainly hear their cry." Deuteronomy 10:18: "He defends the cause of the fatherless and the widow, and loves the foreigner residing among you, giving them food and clothing."

Chapter Fourteen

Transcending Religion to Find Spirituality

When I stand before God at the end of my life, I would hope that I would not have a single bit of talent left, and could say, 'I used everything you gave me'. - Erma Bombeck

Religion, while aiming to unify, often inadvertently perpetuates division, conflict, and segregation. Dr. Martin Luther King Jr. astutely observed, "It is appalling that the most segregated hour of Christian America is eleven o'clock on Sunday morning." Highlighting the stark racial divide in American churches, Dr. King pointed out the contradiction: Christianity, which advocates unity and love, had evident racial schisms. This divide isn't exclusive to Christianity.

For instance, within Jewish practices, an Orthodox Jew might hesitate to enter a Conservative or Reform Synagogue, deeming it against their beliefs. There are those who challenge the Jewish credentials of individuals following these more liberal paths. Even among Orthodox Judaism, differences and tensions exist between sects.

The opening chapter of this book reflects on the opinion of an Orthodox Jewish woman on TikTok, responding to the drama *'Nobody Wants This.'* Her perspective, both assertive and polarizing, declared that individuals identifying as Jewish but not adhering to the strict definitions of the religion as she does are, in her view, not "real Jews" and lack true spirituality.

This perspective introduces a critical tension within the Jewish community and beyond: the intersection of religious identity, practice, and spirituality. It raises profound questions about who defines religious authenticity, how spirituality is understood and expressed, and the diversity of paths within a shared faith tradition.

Sadly, the core of many religious practices often gets buried under doctrines, rituals, and traditions. In this book, we have drawn a distinction between the journey religions prescribe and the ultimate spiritual destination that God hopes for us. While religious teachings primarily steer towards spiritual growth, contemporary practices sometimes divert, emphasizing ritualistic customs over the profound divine connection.

I've noticed an unsettling trend among "spiritual leaders"—Rabbis, Priests, Pastors, other clergy, teachers, and even laypeople—to delegitimize other faiths or factions within their own religion. While this divisive behavior is not new, social media has given marginalized extremists a platform to amplify their voices and spread these harmful messages to a broader audience.

The approach is often the same: they cite scriptural or historical evidence—or more frequently, their specific interpretation of such evidence—to undermine other religions, theologies, or perspectives. This is then followed by an explanation of why their own belief system is superior. What's particularly troubling is seeing educators hold these divisive figures up as role models, embedding this mindset in the next generation.

I firmly believe there is nothing spiritual about this approach. It is self-serving and breeds animosity and division. Instead of building bridges of understanding, it erects walls of distrust and hostility. At its core, this behavior reflects an underlying insecurity in one's own faith, as if the validity of their beliefs hinges on invalidating others.

This divisive mindset originates from the mortal, animalistic soul, which thrives on fear, insecurity, and a need to assert dominance. It has nothing to do with the spiritual soul or the divine spirit within us, which calls us toward love, understanding, and unity. True spirituality is about transcending these base instincts, finding confidence in one's faith without the need to denigrate others. It seeks to unite rather than divide, to inspire rather than alienate, and to reflect the divine attributes of compassion, humility, and grace.

If we, as individuals or as communities, wish to cultivate genuine spirituality, we must reject this divisive tendency. Instead, we should aim to embody the higher attributes of our spiritual soul, fostering respect and dialogue among diverse beliefs. Only by doing so can we rise above the insecurities of our mortal nature and move closer to the divine purpose that unites us all.

> *The ultimate goal of transcending religion is not to weaken faith but to deepen its essence.*

Transcending religion doesn't mean abandoning the rich traditions, beliefs, and rituals that define a faith. It doesn't mean discarding belief in Jesus, the Torah, or other sacred tenets held dear. Nor does it involve delegitimizing other faiths or perspectives. Instead, it calls us to shift our focus toward embodying and reflecting God's attributes—kindness, compassion, restraint, inclusiveness, and mercy.

When we actively live out these divine virtues, we nurture our spiritual souls and refine the base instincts of our mortal selves. This alignment strengthens our connection to The Divine and fosters a society that mirrors God's vision—a world rooted in love, mercy, altruism, and mutual respect.

As we cultivate a deeper spirituality, the boundaries that once divided us begin to blur. Superficial differences lose their significance, and our priorities evolve. In relationships, for instance, we begin to value soulful connections over transient, worldly concerns. The material and fleeting give way to the eternal and spiritual, allowing the immortal soul's light to shine more brightly.

This perspective invites us to reevaluate religious rituals and practices, especially those that exclude or divide based on belief, gender, or other distinctions. The focus shifts from maintaining boundaries to enhancing spirituality, transforming rituals into inclusive practices that foster spiritual growth for all. By adopting this divine lens—seeing the world through the eyes of our spiritual souls rather than our mortal selves—we are challenged to create unity in place of fragmentation, understanding in place of division.

The ultimate goal of transcending religion is not to weaken faith but to deepen its essence. It's about rising above the divides of doctrine and denomination to unify around shared spiritual principles, fostering a collective journey toward The Divine. By doing so, we echo God's attributes in our lives and contribute to a world that embodies compassion, harmony, and grace—a reflection of heaven on earth.

But how do we advance this vision?

Advancing this vision begins with nurturing our spiritual souls and reflecting God's attributes in our lives. Since we are made in God's likeness, we carry the potential to mirror Their divinity. This means choosing compassion over envy, selflessness over selfishness, charity over greed, positivity over negativity, kindness over self-absorption, restraint over impulsiveness, mercy over cruelty, and love over hate. When we consciously embody these virtues, we align with God's purpose and begin shaping a society that reflects Their divine intention.

> *No single religion holds*
> *exclusive claims over the*
> *soul or spirituality.*

God has equipped us with the ability to reflect Their attributes, offering us a blueprint to attain the highest levels of spirituality. Yet, this divine purpose often becomes obscured or distorted by narrow agendas and self-serving interpretations. Many already recognize that true spirituality is not confined to rigid religious observance; it resides within each person as an innate capacity for connection with the divine. No single religion holds exclusive claims over the soul or spirituality, yet some persist in claiming such authority. To advance this vision, we must rise above these limited views, rejecting interpretations that promote exclusion and division.

The path forward lies in emphasizing our immortal souls and God's universal vision for humanity. This approach bridges divides by focusing on what unites us: our shared capacity for spirituality and our collective journey toward divine purpose. The ultimate goal is to recreate the harmony of the Garden of Eden, a state where humanity lived in peace, driven not by fleeting desires or material concerns but by the eternal light of our immortal souls.

In this Edenic vision, humanity thrives in alignment with God's spirit, where kindness, love, and mercy guide our interactions, and division gives way to unity. By choosing to cultivate these divine attributes within ourselves and our communities, we contribute to a world that echoes God's grace—a world where the immortal soul, not the mortal self, defines our priorities and relationships. This is how we advance the vision: by embodying God's love and creating a society that reflects Their eternal harmony.

The Importance of a Spiritual Community

In 1831, Alexis de Tocqueville traveled from France to the United States to try and understand the fledgling democracy being cultivated across the ocean. The result of that travel was what is still considered one of the most important and prolific works ever written on democracy; "Democracy in America." [1] (De Tocqueville, 2004)

Amongst many other observations, Tocqueville noticed the strong individualistic tendencies in American culture. He expressed concerns that extreme individualism might lead to isolation. However, he also recognized that Americans mitigated this through the formation of numerous associations, civil

---

1. De Tocqueville, A. (2004). Alexis de Tocqueville: Democracy in America (LOA #147): A new translation by Arthur Goldhammer. Library of America.

groups, and local political involvement. Tocqueville was surprised by the vital role of religion in a country that maintained a strict separation of church and state. He argued that religion, particularly Protestant Christianity, served as a moral foundation that checked individual excesses and contributed to the nation's stability. Tocqueville was particularly struck by Americans' propensity to form voluntary associations. He noted that when Americans want to advance a cause or address a social issue, they come together to form associations. These groups represented a form of communal action and mutual aid that was distinct from both government intervention and individual effort.

While Tocqueville admired many aspects of American democracy, he also warned of the dangers of excessive individualism. He believed that unchecked individualism could lead to social isolation, diminishing the communal bonds that help hold society together. However, he also noted that Americans combatted this danger by actively fostering civic participation and forming associations, specifically religious groups centered around the church.

Tocqueville's apprehensions seem to have manifested in today's reality. The contemporary American landscape, driven by rampant consumerism, frequently elevates materialistic achievements to paramount importance. Over the past three decades, attendance at churches and synagogues has significantly waned as many young individuals struggle to find spiritual fulfillment within traditional religious frameworks. This declining affiliation, both religious and secular, may be exacerbating the growing feelings of loneliness and isolation observed across developed nations, including the U.S. The collective spirit that once defined American culture seems overshadowed by a surge in individualism. Such a shift towards a more self-focused societal model is precisely what Tocqueville cautioned about, potentially paving the way for the challenges he foresaw regarding the long-term viability of American democracy. This discernible trend is undeniably alarming from various perspectives, although it's beyond the scope of our current study.

Shared goals naturally create a sense of belonging and unity, shifting the focus from individual desires to the collective good.

Thousands of years prior to Tocqueville's travels to America, another event took place that proved the importance of community, and its lessons were very similar to Tocqueville's findings.

In *Exodus 32:19*, the Israelite society descends into chaos, worshiping the Golden Calf and abandoning the communal bonds that had defined them. The Torah describes their state as *parua*—unruly, chaotic, and fragmented. They were no longer a united people but a disordered crowd, each acting on their impulses. To restore order, Moses takes decisive action, not just by quelling the chaos but by offering the Israelites a path to unity and purpose. He gives them two tasks: to observe the Sabbath and to build the Tabernacle.

These specific tasks were not arbitrary; they were deeply intentional. Observing the Sabbath provided the Israelites with a moment of rest and reflection—a chance to pause and reconnect with their spiritual selves and with God. It allowed them to step back from the turmoil and find balance, centering themselves in a rhythm that aligned with divine purpose.

Constructing the Tabernacle, on the other hand, was a collective endeavor. It gave the Israelites a shared mission that required their cooperation, skills, and dedication. Each person contributed in their way—some with materials, others with craftsmanship—fostering a sense of community and collective identity. This communal project redirected their energies toward a divine purpose, symbolized by the Tabernacle, God's dwelling among them.

These two actions—resting together on the Sabbath and working together on the Tabernacle—did more than restore order. They forged a community grounded in spiritual purpose. Shared goals naturally create a sense of belonging and unity, shifting the focus from individual desires to the collective good. This sense of community fosters altruism, encouraging people to act with kindness, generosity, and empathy—qualities that reflect the immortal, spiritual soul rather than the mortal, animalistic soul.

Alexis de Tocqueville would later observe a similar phenomenon, noting that communities built on shared values and mutual support reduce reliance on external authority and serve as a safeguard against despotism. A strong, spiritually driven community embodies divine attributes and enriches the spiritual lives of its members, countering the isolation and self-centeredness that individualism often breeds.

As we strive to cultivate a spiritual society, the lessons from this episode in Exodus remain profoundly relevant. A community grounded in shared spiritual values can transcend sectarian boundaries, emphasizing inclusivity and spirituality over division. At the heart of such a society lies a collective pursuit of spiritual altruism—a commitment to the well-being of others that magnifies the spirituality of each individual.

By building communities that prioritize shared purpose and spiritual growth, we reflect the divine attributes of compassion, unity, and love. In doing so, we align ourselves with God's vision for humanity, creating a society that nurtures the immortal soul and uplifts all its members. This collective pursuit not only strengthens us as individuals but also transforms us into a people worthy of carrying the divine presence within and among us.

Spiritual Altruism

Spiritual altruism calls us to emphasize unity and inclusion, transcending divisions without undermining individual religious beliefs or practices—unless those practices foster division, selfishness, or other traits rooted in the mortal soul. Personal convictions, whether grounded in the teachings of Jesus, the commandments of the Torah, or any other sacred tradition, remain deeply significant to their adherents. These beliefs and customs offer unique and irreplaceable pathways to connect with The Divine. Rather than seeking to replace them, spiritual altruism seeks to enhance them, infusing traditions with added spiritual meaning that resonates with a modern generation yearning for spirituality yet firmly rooted in their religious heritage.

By prioritizing spiritual altruism over purely ritualistic religious practices, we open ourselves to enriched ways of experiencing The Divine. This shift encourages inclusivity and compassion while moving away from doctrines that create barriers. When we begin to see humanity through the lens of the immortal spiritual soul, our cherished traditions don't lose value; instead, they are rejuvenated with new purpose and deeper meaning.

Spiritual altruism offers a chance to redefine and deepen religious practices.

Take, for example, interfaith couples navigating the complex task of harmonizing their diverse religious backgrounds. These couples often aim to provide equal representation of both faiths, exposing their children to a blend of traditions. A child might attend church services on Easter and Christmas while also lighting candles during Chanukah or celebrating a bar mitzvah. While these efforts can foster a sense of inclusivity, they sometimes focus on the form rather than the spiritual substance, leaving children with a superficial understanding of these practices or even a sense of confusion about their spiritual identity.

Rather than settling for a simple amalgamation of rituals, spiritual altruism offers a chance to redefine and deepen these traditions. It's not about compromise but about reimagining rituals as conduits for profound spiritual significance. Faith declarations that, once excluded or divided, can evolve into affirmations of our shared spiritual journey and humanity's collective potential for awakening to higher purpose.

This approach doesn't negate or replace traditional religious frameworks but expands their scope. It offers a vision of spiritual harmony that respects and honors diverse beliefs while cultivating a shared mission. While established religious institutions may resist this evolution, spiritual altruism is uniquely positioned to unite individuals from various backgrounds under a collective spiritual ambition.

By reinterpreting religious traditions in light of God's benevolent attributes—compassion, mercy, and love—we create a richer, more inclusive spiritual experience. This approach offers a glimpse of humanity's potential when aligned with God's primordial intent: a world where traditions and beliefs converge to reflect the unity, purpose, and divine grace that transcend all divides. It paints a hopeful picture of what we can become when we place spiritual growth and harmony at the heart of our existence.

The Meaning of Life

In 2020, a Gallup poll[2] studied membership in various houses of worship, including churches, synagogues, and mosques. The findings reaffirmed what regular attendees had been observing: only 47% of Americans were part of a religious institution, a decline from the 73% recorded when Gallup first investigated this in 1937. This percentage remained relatively unchanged for about six decades.

---

2. (Gallup, 2021) https://news.gallup.com/poll/341963/church-membership-falls-below-majority-first-time.aspx

Gallup noted, "The decline in church membership chiefly stems from the growing number of Americans who claim no religious affiliation. From 8% in 1998-2000, this segment increased to 13% in 2008-2010 and then to 21% in the most recent three years."

Between 1998 and 2020, a consistent decline in membership was evident across all denominations, religious affiliations, demographics, political stances, and geographical areas. Although specific figures about the number of church and synagogue closures in the past twenty years aren't readily available, a discernible trend emerges with the dwindling church-attending population, primarily comprising baby boomers.

These findings align with post-COVID research. [3] Springtide Research Institute, a neutral non-profit entity, discovered that 77% of Gen Z individuals consider themselves spiritual, with 68% identifying as religious.

When asked about belief in a 'Higher Power'—a broad term not limited to Christian or any religious interpretation—about one-third of individuals aged 18-25 affirmed their belief.

Many of these young adults clarified that while they might not subscribe to classical or biblical views of God, they do believe in some superior force or intelligence. Gen Z seems

---

3. (Springtide Research, 2022)
   https://www.springtideresearch.org/product/the-state-of
   -religion-young-people-2022-mental-health

less inclined toward organized religion despite their heightened spiritual consciousness.

Post-COVID[4], church attendance hasn't regained its former levels. Instead, it saw a decline, especially as the virus hit older generations—typical church-goers—harder than their younger counterparts.

The data presents a clear narrative: younger generations remain as spiritually inclined as their predecessors, but they're not resonating with traditional religious establishments. Instead, they seem to be on a quest for spirituality, connection to a Higher Power, and communal well-being, suggesting an inclination towards activities that foster spiritual enrichment.

A 2017 Gallup investigation into church attendance motivations found the majority cited sermons, youth-oriented spiritual programs, community outreach, and volunteer opportunities as the main reasons. These results correlate with the spiritual aspects of what a younger generation is asking for in religious observance.

The ground is fertile for spiritual growth and a religious reimagination. This revolution doesn't happen globally, nationally, or even locally. It starts very modestly, with a few families, a small community getting together and agreeing to make change through common spiritual goals. It happens amongst interfaith families looking for a blended spiritual and religious

---

4. (Gallup, 2023) https://news.gallup.com/poll/507692/church-attendance-lower-pre-pandemic.aspx

experience away from the rigid conventional religious institutes. It happens with young people looking to express themselves spiritually without the rigid doctrine of institutionalized religious organizations. It happens amongst the marginalized communities looking for spiritual equality. It happens with the LGBTQI+ communities looking for acceptance and representation in religion in place of exclusion and persecution.

Young people are breaking down the social and religious barriers established by generations of religious division. They are blurring the traditional divisions and looking for a spiritual experience that is meaningful, inclusive, and universal. They are no less religious or spiritual than their ancestors; they believe in God or a Higher Power but search for a spiritual experience transcending institutionalized religion.

This vision of spirituality is not a utopia; it is within our grasp. As is written in Deuteronomy:

> *Surely, this Instruction which I enjoin upon you this day is not too baffling for you, nor is it beyond reach. It is not in the heavens, that you should say, "Who among us can go up to the heavens and get it for us and impart it to us, that we may observe it?" Neither is it beyond the sea, that you should say, "Who among us can cross to the other side of the sea and get it for us and impart it to us, that we may observe it?" No, the thing is very close to you, in your mouth and in your heart, to observe it. See,*

*I set before you this day life and prosperity, death
and adversity.*

Deuteronomy 30: 11 - 15

Believing in a Higher Power invites us to live a life filled with mercy, compassion, positivity, and selflessness. It calls us to apply justice tempered with mercy, recognizing that each of us walks a unique path, playing our role in the divine plan. By embracing the idea of a spiritual community and understanding that we connect to the divine through our immortal souls, we unlock a deeper awareness of life's purpose.

This life is fleeting, but how we live it has profound implications for our immortal souls. By striving to elevate our immortal spiritual essence above the instincts of our mortal, earthly selves, we align with the ultimate purpose of life: spirituality. This belief—that the meaning of life is ultimate spirituality—brings us closer to The Divine's plan for humanity.

Respecting religious traditions and beliefs need not confine us within the boundaries of exclusion. Instead, we can transcend above religion to find spiritual commonality—a shared connection to The Divine that bridges divisions and unites us in our collective purpose. By mirroring divine attributes such as love, kindness, compassion, and mercy, we foster a society rooted in the love of humanity. This love, in turn, nurtures our spirituality, allowing it to permeate every aspect of our lives.

This vision offers humanity a new paradigm for realizing spirituality. It shifts the focus from rigid dogma to a universal pursuit of divine connection. It provides a fresh framework for understanding spirituality, one that echoes God's original intent when They created the Garden of Eden—a harmonious, unified existence where humanity reflected the divine attributes in all their actions.

By believing and living this vision, we can co-create a world that aligns with God's eternal purpose—a world where love, unity, and spirituality flourish, reminding us of our shared divine origin and destiny.

Epilogue

Throughout my life, I have amazed myself time and time again. I've consistently surpassed my own expectations. I have faced so many towering mountains that I had to climb. I could have easily selected an easier path that led in a different direction away from the challenges of life; however, every time I faced a challenge, I climbed that mountain and overcame the obstacle. In doing so, I amazed myself at my achievement and credited my success to a Higher Power that helped me. In reality, it might have been a Higher Power that brought me to the doorstep of the mountain, but it was I alone who had to climb it. Looking back at the mountain I had climbed, I was thankful to The Divine for presenting me with the challenge and proud of myself, maybe more than anything else, amazed at myself for achieving something I had only recently believed was impossible for me.

Whether in achieving physical, academic, professional, or life goals, I climbed each mountain as it crossed my path. I didn't deviate from the life path I was on, and I didn't run away, choose a shortcut, or choose an easier path; I met my challenges head-on and remained faithful to the course I was on.

Today, I continue along this chosen path, continually surprising myself with the obstacles I overcome and the success I attain. Where it leads, I don't know. However, I know this is the path The Divine has placed me on and guided me down. Everywhere I look, I see signs reinforcing this belief: the inspiring people I meet, serendipitous encounters that transform my life, unexpected rewards, and gentle nudges from The Divine that keep me centered. All these are affirmations that The Divine designates a path for each and every one of us; whether we choose to follow that path is our personal decision - our free will. However, I believe that the rewards for doing so are manifested in our lives and, specifically, in our immortal spiritual souls.

> What is genuine spirituality, and how can we achieve it?

This was the question I asked at the start of this journey. If, after reading this, your answer still relies on the exclusivity of your own religion—if it dismisses or marginalizes others and reduces spirituality to the traditions and rituals you've inherited—then the ideas in this book have not yet fully taken root in your consciousness.

By learning to view life through the lens of the immortal spiritual soul, I've offered you a new perspective on what The Divine wishes from humanity. When we recognize that each and every one of us has a role to play in God's greater plan, we naturally move from exclusion to inclusion.

No single religion can claim to have sole authority over God or the "only path" to salvation. All faiths, in their own ways, guide seekers toward a Higher Power. Some follow Jesus, others honor the Torah's laws, still others obey the Prophet Muhammad's teachings, or follow various philosophies. Yet the shared aim across all traditions remains the same: to unite with the divine presence. Sadly, many religious factions insist they alone possess the true roadmap to heaven, a narrow-minded stance that harms our collective spiritual potential. This book strives to articulate the soul's spiritual aspirations, independent of religious labels, and shows how religion can serve as a powerful vehicle for spiritual growth when approached with the right mindset.

From the earliest scriptures, God has shown us the kind of behavior They desire—teaching us spirituality, endowing us with divine attributes, and creating us in Their image. Looking at Jesus' teachings reveals that he understood the Torah's vision. Across all religions, the pursuit of ultimate spirituality is essentially a pursuit of love.

Instead of entrenching ourselves in religious boundaries, we must tear down the walls that divide us. The antidote to exclusion is inclusion. Embracing the full spectrum of faiths, cultures, ethnicities, orientations, and beliefs weaves a vibrant tapestry of humanity united by a single goal: to deepen our collective spirituality and realize the divine plan.

I have walked my path in faithfulness, and my soulmate has walked hers with unwavering belief and determination. Our

separate journeys, shaped by different landscapes, finally con-
verged at a destined crossroads. In that moment, we recognized
the subtle divine weaving that brought us together. Our two
distinct roads have now merged into one unified highway. Hand
in hand, we face life's challenges, guided by trust and love. We
pray our shared journey will inspire humanity to build a society
that reflects the divine vision.

This vision is both deeply personal and universally human.
It's not so distant that we must cross oceans to find it, nor
so high that we must ascend into the heavens. It's within our
reach—right here. This is the divine blueprint for humanity:
a path to ultimate spirituality and ultimate love. It is the core
aspiration of all religions, the hope of restoring Eden's harmony
on Earth.

Gideon Paull,
Los Angeles, December 2024.

Bibliography

American Psychiatric Association, DSM-5 Task Force. (2013). *Diagnostic and statistical manual of mental disorders: DSM-5™ (5th ed.)*. American Psychiatric Publishing.

Avenevoli, S. S. (2015). Major depression in the National Comorbidity Survey–Adolescent Supplement: prevalence, correlates, and treatment. *Journal of the American Academy of Child & Adolescent Psychiatry, 54(1)*, 37-44.

Bandura, A. (1977). Self-efficacy: Toward a unifying theory of behavioral change. *Psychological Review, 84(2)*, 191-215.

Bantas, H. (2010). *Understanding Plato: 'The Symposium*. Hercules Bantas.

Bar-El, Y. D. (2000). Jerusalem syndrome. *The British Journal of Psychiatry*, 86-90.

Birnbaum, G. E. (2018). The fragile spell of desire: a functional perspective on changes in sexual desire across relationship development. *Personality and Social Psychology Review,*, 101-127.

Brodt, K. (2020, October 29). *The Legends of Lincoln's Ghost.* Retrieved from Boundary Stones: https://boundarystones.weta.org/2020/10/29/legends-lincolns-ghost

Calvin, J. B. (2017). *Institutes of the Christian religion.* Hendrickson Publishers.

De Tocqueville, A. (2004). *Democracy in America* . Library of America.

Descartes, R. (1641). *Meditations on First Philosophy.*

Eliade, M. (1982). *Ordeal by Labyrinth.* Univ of Chicago Pr; First US Edition (January 1, 1982).

Freud, S. (1923). *The Ego and the Id.* The Hogarth Press Ltd.

Freud, S. (1989). *The Future of an Illusion.* W. W. Norton & Company; The Standard edition (September 17, 1989).

Freud, S. (1990). *New Introductory Lectures on Psycho-Analysis.* W. W. Norton & Company; The Standard edition (February 17, 1990).

Gallup. (2021, March 29). *U.S. Church Membership Falls Below Majority for First Time.* Retrieved from Gallup: https://news.gallup.com/poll/341963/church-membership-falls-below-majority-first-time.aspx

Gallup. (2023, June 26). *U.S. Church Attendance Still Lower Than Pre-Pandemic.* Retrieved from Gallup: https://news.gallup.com/poll/507692/church-attendance-lower-pre-pandemic.aspx

Goleman, D. (2012). *Emotional Intelligence: Why It Can Matter More Than IQ Emotional Intelligence: Why It Can Matter More Than IQ.* Bantam; 1st edition (January 11, 2012).

Leiden, U. (2017, March 27). *The importance of relating to others: Why we only learn to understand other people after the age of four.* Retrieved from Science Daily: https://www.sciencedaily.com/releases/2017/03/170327083433.htm

Maimonides, M. (2000). *The Guide for the Perplexed: Revised edition.* Dover Publications.

Mann, W. E. (2015). *God, modality, and morality.* Oxford University Press.

McCready, A. (2016). *The Me, Me, Me Epidemic: A Step-by-Step Guide to Raising Capable, Grateful Kids in an Over-Entitled World.* . Penguin.

McLeod, S. (2023, July 10). *Freud's Theory Of Personality: Id, Ego, And Superego.* Retrieved from Simply Psychology: https://www.simplypsychology.org/psyche.html

Orth, U. R. (2009). Disentangling the effects of low self-esteem and stressful events on depression: Findings from three longitudinal studies. *Journal of Personality and Social Psychology, 97(2),* 307–321.

Parel, A. J. (2007). *Gandhi's Philosophy and the Quest for Harmony.* Cambridge University Press; 1st edition (December 17, 2007).

Pinker, S. (2003). *The Blank Slate: The Modern Denial of Human Nature.* Penguin Press Science.

Shariff, A. &. (2012). *Divergent effects of beliefs in heaven and hell on national crime rates.* Retrieved from PLOS: https://doi.org/10.1371/journal.pone.0039048

Siddle, R. H. (2002). Religious delusions in patients admitted to hospital with schizophrenia. *Social psychiatry and psychiatric epidemiology*, 130-138.

Springtide Research. (2022). *The State of Religion & Young People 2022: Mental Health–What Faith Leaders Need to Know.* Retrieved from Sprintide Research Institute: https://www.springtideresearch.org/product/the-state-of-religion-young-people-2022-mental-health

Steinsaltz. (2018). *The Soul.* Jerusalem: Maggid.

Sternberg, R. J. (2004). *The Psychology Of Hate.* Amer Psychological Assn; 1st edition (January 1, 2004).

Viding E, M. E. (2018). Understanding the development of psychopathy: progress and challenges. *Psycol Med.*, 566-577.

Watson, K. M. (2013). *The Class Meeting.* Seedbed Publishing.

Wiesel, E. (2006). *Night.* Hill and Wang. (Original work published 1956).

Woolger, R. (2004). *Beyond Death: Transition and the Afterlife* . Retrieved from Royal College of Psychiatrists : https://www.rcpsych.ac.uk/docs/default-source/members/sigs/spirituality-spsig/att89154-att.pdf?sfvrsn=8da39ec7_2

Woolger, R. J. (2004). *Beyond Death: Transition and the Afterlife.* Retrieved from Royal College of Psychiatrists: https://www.rcpsych.ac.uk/docs/default-source/members/sigs/spirituality-spsig/att89154-att.pdf?sfvrsn=8da39ec7_2

About the Author

Gideon, who grew up in a traditional Jewish home and proudly practices his Judaism, is married to Elaine, an ordained pastor for the United Methodist Church in Southern California. Together, they believe that we are all children of God and can connect on the level of the soul instead of the established physical, cultural, or religious groupings that tend to segregate and divide us. The experience of finding each other and living a blended life where the beliefs and values of each other are valued and combined has opened their eyes to the possibilities of a world where religious boundaries are broken down, and respectful coexistence becomes the accepted norm.

Gideon credits much of his understanding of the soul, the spirit, and God to his marriage to Elaine; together, they openly explore their spirituality and attempt to decipher what God is asking of each of us. Instead of focusing on religious differences, they attempt to find commonality and promote spiritual compatibility in place of religious compatibility.

Gideon grew up in a Jewish home in Windsor, England, where education, Jewish practice, and coexistence were fundamental values. His experiences growing up Jewish, in a place almost devoid of fellow Jews, enabled him to accept and respect other religions. Living in The United Kingdom, Israel, France, and the United States has shaped Gideon's understanding of cultural and religious differences and given him respect for those who use their religion to better humanity. He believes that all religions walk a spiritual path that leads them to God. Gideon and his wife, Elaine, strongly believe that regardless of religion, we find more commonality than differences when we work towards a shared spiritual goal.

Gideon holds a degree in Mechanical Engineering and now spends his time developing complex web applications and working with companies to improve their engineering business processes. In his spare time, he enjoys writing, studying scripture, endless spiritual discussions with his wife, Elaine, and writing alternative commentaries to the Torah. Staying active, Gideon enjoys cycling, hiking, working out, and traveling. Gideon is father to four children and, at the time of writing, six grandchildren.

www.ingramcontent.com/pod-product-compliance
Lightning Source LLC
Chambersburg PA
CBHW021230130626
46554CB00004B/1422